Down To Earth Management

Down To Earth Management

A Guide For Real Life Managers

Robert M. Coquillette

Writer's Showcase

San Jose New York Lincoln Shanghai

Down To Earth Management
A Guide For Real Life Managers

Writer's Showcase
an imprint of iUniverse.com, Inc.

For information address:
iUniverse.com, Inc.
5220 S 16th, Ste. 200
Lincoln, NE 68512
www.iuniverse.com

ISBN: 0-595-16969-4

Printed in the United States of America

This book is dedicated to my wife, Dagmar,
who was always there through thick and thin
and to the many friends whose insight, comment and criticism
helped make this volume so much more useful.

CONTENTS

How to get started now that you are the boss. How to behave on the first day. What you should learn from the previous incumbent. Should the secretary or assistant you inherited be fired? The first general meeting. Important early plans.

How to get the people for whom you are responsible to do what you want them to do. Can the boss be a bastard and still get results? What is the right way and the wrong way to discipline? What are the five basic options for discipline? How to make every contact with your people count.

Discovering the essence of every organization. the five basic categories of employees and what this means to the manager. The required "state of mind" for the manager. Three aspects of the manager's job. The importance of anticipation. What you have the right to expect from your people and what they have the right to expect from you.

PREFACE

This book was written to answer the needs of those persons who have recently taken on management responsibilities although it should help the more experienced manager to do a better job. It is meant to be especially useful to the professional specialist: the lawyer, the chemist, the financial analyst, the salesman, the teacher, the computer programmer who has been given management responsibilities. Many enter a career path as a professional specialist right out of school and when promoted to a management position find they have little experience or training in what it means to be "the boss". Although this guide deals mainly with the commercial or business world in mind, other persons such as teachers or social workers when making the transition from specialist to a management position will find this guide just as practical. An enterprise is an enterprise whether run for profit or not and the manager of any enterprise is faced with many of the same problems. This, then, is a book about the practical, down-to-earth aspects of being a manager or "executive", of being **THE Boss** to a group of people.

The manager's job is different in a number of ways from that of the technical professional. To begin with it covers a great number of somewhat unrelated skills ranging all the way from how to actually tell people what to do to how to handle the media. The specific content of the job is not so well defined as in other activities. It is easy to answer the child's question, "What do you do at the office?" if one is a doctor or a computer programmer. It is far more difficult when one is a "manager". This book deals with many of the detailed actions or skills one needs as a manager, skills which are broadly applicable and come more from experience than from professional training. Much of what is included here has application at any level of management since every position has certain elements of every other position in it, only the scale or the circumstances change. Likewise the same elements are found in small organizations as well as large. While many of the examples used in the book are drawn from experience in large organizations, the same principles apply in the small organization although at times not so clearly defined. Being a good executive is *not* being brilliant. A good executive or manager is rather consistent, responsible, predictable, skillful. This is a question of craftsmanship...of the same dedication and excellence one expects of the professional athlete or artist. It is the execution of the elements of the job with the same snap and timing one expects of the "pro" of any calling. One can't be stupid and be a good manager, but brains or brilliance are only a part of the total equation. Common sense and an appreciation of the qualities of others are even more important.

The book is divided into four parts. Part one deals with skills specific to the manager. The second section covers working with others in the organization including the manager's own boss. The third section is directed at the manager's own career as an individual rather than as a representative of the position and the subjects are of general use regardless of the position. Finally part four has a couple of chapters about traveling and about doing business overseas written in deference to the increasingly international nature of many enterprises plus a chapter on how to look at physical facilities. These chapters should be especially useful to anyone sent on an overseas mission or thinking about going abroad.

One final word of prologue. The work of the world is mostly done by ordinary people, and the essence of a successful, commercial or institutional venture is repetitive performance, i.e. doing the required work up to standard day after day. Thus the first secret of successful management is never to make a decision or structure a job which cannot be executed by ordinary human beings realizing that in most cases these persons will be called on to do essentially the same thing week after week. As a manager or executive, one needs to have a great many skillful, but ordinary people who can be depended on to carry out the many individual, repetitive actions of a going enterprise, motivated to execute those tasks so competently and consistently as to assure its success. This can be a challenging assignment for the manager, but it is not the work of genius. Today's manager has another element which complicates his or her job. Any enterprise is a fine balance of a number of related factors. Under stable conditions the optimum balance is often reached over time by trial and error. In this day and age the conditions under which the enterprise functions tend to be quite unstable from both internal and external pressures. One key management task thus becomes the management of change: change in the technologies being used, change in political atmosphere and regulation, change in competitive forces and change in the attitudes of people. This book is a manual of practical ways to master the demands of a job where many of its facets are as old as human nature and others are as fresh as today's news.

Women are increasingly active in management positions and this guide should be especially useful to women who are just coming into management. It is a little awkward to always write "he or she" thus the reader should keep in mind that the thoughts and methods described in the chapters which follow apply regardless of gender.

Robert M. Coquillette
Mattapoisett, MA November, 2000

Part I

SOME PRACTICAL MANAGEMENT SKILLS

CHAPTER 1

SO NOW YOU'RE THE BOSS

Let's get right into it! You have been made manager of ___. No matter what the title or how it is announced, a group of people are now looking at you as "The New Boss". They are asking each other, "What kind of a boss will this person be?" They will be hanging on every word you say. They will be looking for clues and even though you may have been around the shop or office for some time, all of a sudden you will be looked at in a different light. Some will even be asking why **YOU** got the job instead of X or Y who are better qualified in their opinion! This may not be a new experience for you, but no matter how many times you have taken over a new position first steps and first impressions are important. There are certain basic rules that apply to any new position whether you're to be the boss or not, but as the boss they are particularly critical. The farther up the ladder the new position takes you, the more important these initial moves may be.

FIRST THINGS FIRST!

Be conservative in your dress on the first day but don't make any great change from what you have been accustomed to wear. Everyone will be looking to see how you have reacted to the new position.

Just be pleasant with everyone. There is plenty of time later to start being efficient. But *listen* to what people are saying because there may be some important messages you should hear.

Don't speculate about what you might do or what "reforms"you have in mind. On the other hand don't assure people that "everything is going to be the same". People are going to read into any pronouncement by the new boss much more than he or she ever intended. So "mind your tongue" since the staff is going to take very seriously indeed anything you say. Just remember what the press does to a new president of the United States!

Do be careful about setting the stage for the little things such as how you intend to address your assistant/secretary, what you do about the coffee-break, how long you take for lunch, what time you quit work at night. People will be watching for indicators long before you make and announce any formal decisions.

Get around to meet or to say hello to everyone. Make it a point for the first few days to greet people as you come and go. Again, they will all be looking for indicators as to the kind of relationship the boss wants to establish. You want to be friendly without being too "buddy-buddy". If you have been promoted out of the group, try to be just a bit more formal without becoming a stuffed shirt or being accused of the new position having gone to your head. Mostly it's a matter of just being pleasant.

Let your group know that you expect everyone to continue doing his or her job as usual. Remind them that any problems should be brought to your attention promptly. They may need to know that you want to be "bothered" when there are problems.

WHAT YOU SHOULD LEARN FROM THE PREVIOUS INCUMBENT

One of the most valuable sources of information, (regardless of what you may think about the capabilities of the previous person on the job which you have just taken over), is the previous incumbent. Even if you have to go to considerable effort to get some of his (or her) time it is well worth the trouble. Even more important is preparing for the questions you want him or her to answer for you. Take along a pad of paper and make notes. Remember that you want the previous boss to "tell all" so get the person talking and just listen to what he or she is telling you whether or not you agree or approve.

> Perhaps the best way to get the ball rolling is to ask what the previous person sees as the most important future issue. There may be more than one and that's OK, too. If you don't understand the issue or its significance, be sure to ask plenty of questions so you do.

> Another subject to be explored is what the person considers the "most successful" program of the recent past. It goes without saying that you should find out why it was considered successful.

> It's an easy step to "What problems have you been working on during the last six months?" This discussion is bound to bring in relationships with other departments and this subject should be explored in appropriate depth.

> The previous topic also leads to an important subject and that is advice in dealing with peers and other officials in the hierarchy. Again, the clue here is to listen and understand regardless of what your own thoughts may be.

While you may have been in the organization for a long time and even may have been put into the job because your predecessor couldn't get along with the hierarchy, what he tells you may give some important clues about this particular position. You are in a new position and your relationships change, too.

Just one word of warning—*DON'T GOSSIP.* Especially if you have been around the organization for a while, there is a tendency to get chummy on a subject like this one. Don't! Just listen and keep your own counsel.

Now for a subject that will take some time. What you want is an evaluation of all the people who will be reporting to you and of others in the organization whose capabilities the previous manager thinks you should know. You also want his comment about each individual's salary level. This is best done with the salary records in front of you so you can be talking specific figures and not generalities. You should look for and question obvious abnormal or out-of-line situations such as no raise for several years or increases that are out of the pattern for the group as a whole.

More than any other single record, what has actually happened to salaries will reveal the dynamics of the group you are about to supervise. If written performance reviews exist, look at them in relation to the salary history.

As a special case, you should ask for a candid evaluation of the personal secretary or assistant if you are to inherit his. Take enough time on this one so that it all comes out because whether or not to retain that person will be one of the early decisions you will have to make.

Finally you need to know about the confidential files. Where are they? Who has access to them? What do they cover? Are they all in place or is your predecessor going to take some or all of them with him? If the files are to go, you should review them promptly and make copies of anything you may need. If they are in the computer or on a diskette, be sure you can get at them.

GETTING STARTED WITH THE STAFF

The whole purpose of the exercise which follows is for you to learn how the unit **really works**. To start you have to find out who is working in the department or division, *all of them.* This means you have to get a complete roster preferably one with the salary history included. You may think you know who is working in the unit especially if you have been a part of it, but *do not assume.* If you reviewed salaries with the previous incumbent, check to see that the list that person used checks with what you have now been given. You also need an organization chart and this should be the "official" chart if there is one in existence. In the small organization, you may have to draw up your own.

Compare what the salary roster says with what the organization chart shows and make sure you understand any differences especially if titles don't seem to be the same.

Determine who the key people are and ask each of them to write up a brief job description showing:

Title
Principle Function
Responsibilities including those persons reporting to him or to her.
Authorities as specifically as possible.

Sit down with each of these key people and talk about the description enough so you understand the way each position functions. Be careful in your comments not to approve the description. At this point all you are trying to do is understand what each person thinks his or her job is.

Have each key person take the list of the people reporting to him or to her and put down a brief description of the function and a simple statement about the capability of each person. You may wish to do the latter orally, but in either case the evaluation should be checked against any formal record and against the salary history.

NOW IT'S YOUR TURN IN THE BOX

All of the above should not take more than a couple of days, but even in that short time people are going to expect that you are on the job and functioning. Don't be surprised though if it seems as though there isn't anything to do although all your people seem to be busy and carrying on the department's work with little or no input from you. Most day-to-day activity is quite routine and your people will take care of it until a problem comes up. Just let it go like that because you can use the time. If someone comes to you for a decision it's best to start with, "What do you usually do in a case like this?" or "What has the past practice been?" Don't rush into making operating decisions until you understand how the game is played! Someone may be trying to embarrass you. If you need to get an answer from someone else, don't hesitate to do so. Tell the employee you'll get back to them by saying something like, "I'll check that out for you and get back to you this afternoon." Then, do it! If you promise an answer at a later time, always follow up otherwise your people will lose confidence in you.

Concentrate on learning the vocabulary used in the institution and use it as much as you can. Again, even though you may be an old-timer around the place, in this particular group there may be a local "dialect" of words or phrases that are special.

Begin thinking about the decision that has to be made with regard to your chief secretary and/or executive assistant if you inherited one with the job. The decision to replace, if necessary, has to be made in not more than 30 days. If the person has to go, by getting it done promptly it will be understood as part of the change in the position. If you wait for three or four months and then decide a change has to be made, you will have to go through the entire procedure of warning, developing the case and finally terminating or demoting the person. (See the chapter on "Dealing With People You Supervise") In other words, after about the first month the people you inherited with the job are *yours* and if there are problems you will have to handle them as though you had been around for years.

With all the information gleaned from the job descriptions and the organization chart, decide on the future organization and job content for the key positions. Don't do anything about this just yet. It may require modification as you see how the group actually performs.

Based on your own goals and on what you have learned in talking with the past incumbent and with your people draw up a list of not more than *five* goals for the year ahead. This will help you as you think about people and organization.

Call a staff meeting with your key people to which they are to come prepared to discuss the work plan for the next three months as specifically as possible. It is particularly important to get deadline dates when specific actions must be taken or completed. This can be done under the excuse that you are "learning" and need to know what has to be done. Don't make a big deal out of this especially in the small organization, but it is a good way to find out what others think is important. In this meeting make a point of saying that you will share with them any information you get which will affect them and you expect they will do the same with you. What you want to do is establish a policy of "open lines" between you and your people. You also want people to know that you *expect* to be kept informed of any and all job-related problems. No one should be able to say, "I didn't know you wanted to know about little problems."

One final word. It is important that you keep your own counsel at this point. Everyone is watching to see what the new boss is going to do and how he is going to do it. Again, don't speculate out loud. People will take anything you say very seriously and read into it much that is not there. Don't talk about how things were done in the company or institution from which you came (with the implied thought that the previous method was superior!). Stick with the facts and do a lot of consulting and listening. Let the others do the talking until all of the skeletons come out of the closets. You will have plenty of time to make your mark as the weeks roll by. Don't joke about your predecessor or about the way things are done. Jokes have a way of turning into disasters!

ACTIONS REQUIRED

There are a few specific actions which any new boss must take. While they are generally implied in the sections above, the following list is a useful reminder.

> A general staff meeting should be held within the first couple of days just to say that you are glad to be working in their unit and that you expect everyone will continue to do his job while you learn "the ropes". Stress that you want to know about problems as soon as they occur and you want people to feel free to come to you.

Within the first two weeks you must make time to sit down individually with each of your key people to review with them what they are doing and what their work plans are.(This in addition to the staff meeting called for above.)

You must determine immediately how you are to report to your boss and just what method of communication he or she prefers. Sit down and talk specifically about this point. Some like a scheduled daily or weekly session. Some prefer to get reports in writing with the idea they'll call you if they want more discussion. This is one of the things you should have found out from your predecessor, but check it out with *your* boss. Maybe your predecessor didn't have it right.

As pointed out above, within the first month you must determine if your personal secretary/staff assistant needs replacement and start the necessary steps.

Within three months you must determine which other personnel must be replaced and set up a schedule with which your boss should concur.

Within three months working with the job descriptions and your target organization chart, you should make such changes in job content as are required and see that those individuals affected by the changes truly understand what you want.

You must get a clear picture of what *your* boss expects from putting you in the new position. If you got the job in spite of his wishes (which happens in large institutions) it is even more important to find out just what you can do to make your boss glad he's got you. There's a great temptation to try to prove that one is excellent by working to one's own agenda. There will be plenty of time for that after you know what the boss's agenda is!

You must establish a way of communicating with your people in a routine way which usually means establishing a "staff meeting" or perhaps a weekly "manager's letter" if the group is spread out. In addition you will want to meet or talk regularly with some of the individuals who are key to the operation. Just as you need to know how your boss wants you to communicate with him, let those who work for you know what you want from them. Just tell them. They want to know.

Get familiar with the manuals, procedures, regulations and other written material which apply to your unit. This is best done as "homework" so you don't have to take time away from the daily job. When you find places where actual practice doesn't seem to fit what you read, ask questions. As Macchiavelli wrote, "A prince is a great asker of questions." Actually, this practice is good for many situations. Just keep asking questions until you are sure you understand the circumstances before making a judgement.

Taking on a new job is mostly a matter of good sense. The people whom you will be supervising really want you to succeed because your success insures theirs. Once the initial lull when the unit seems to run itself is over, you will find that there may not be enough hours in the day to do what seems to be needed. By that time you should have your team and your plans in place so you are working with as much going for you as possible. Don't worry about whether you will be able to do the job. It has been done by someone no better than you! Just focus on doing first things first, piece by piece, rather than fretting about the whole big task. This nervous energy is better devoted to getting the work done! "Rome was not built in a day".

CHAPTER 2

THE ART OF SUPERVISING

The manager's job is to supervise those persons working for him. Seems like a pretty simple task yet volumes have already been written on the subject. In this chapter, I propose to outline a few practical and tested elements which make the successful boss—successful. It will mainly be suggestions about how *you* are to behave. As a manager, one's behavior and attitudes are watched constantly by those being supervised. There is no way for the boss to take time off from this fact. Company lore is full of tales about what the boss did at the company party when he or she got a few drinks aboard, at the very party which was supposed to demonstrate that the boss and the employees were all just one big happy family. So the first rule in dealing with employees is, "Recognize that you *are* the boss and conduct yourself accordingly at all times when in the presence of those whom you supervise". It is significant that the great enduring examples of management, namely the military and the Catholic Church insist that "conduct becoming to an officer" is the only acceptable standard.

Of course this leads to the question,"How does one behave as a boss to get the optimum response, and respect, from those being supervised?". First of all one must be *consistent*. Those you supervise need to be able to predict your behavior. It has often been said it is perfectly possible to work with and even admire a predictable bastard! It is the person who is charming one day and a tyrant the next with whom one is unable to cope. You can be sure employees watch the boss as he or she comes and goes trying to fathom the mood the boss is in and what news he or she may be carrying. In large offices or factory departments the rumors fly: "Is it a lay-off?" "Have we lost a big contract?" "Did our boss just get eaten-out by the *big boss*?"...and so it goes. Not because the employees have any great compassion, but rather because they are constantly concerned about the effect on their *own* lives. Knowing this, one must always maintain a friendly, even-tempered appearance to the world-at-large regardless of how things are going. Your people should be able to depend on you to be the calm, steady one and the one who maintains a good disposition no matter what the circumstances.

Perhaps as important as plain consistency in dealing with people is consistent fair-play and even-handedness. There is no place for favoritism in being a good manager. Each person must be treated with the respect and dignity owed every human being. That doesn't mean that failure should be ignored when performance or behavior doesn't meet standards or expectations. It does mean that all persons should be held to the same standards, and correction or discipline should be done privately or in such a way that the person's dignity is preserved.

As pointed out in the forward to this book, the work of the world is mostly done by ordinary people and the successful manager never forgets this truth. In giving orders or in setting out work to be done he or she will be certain the employee understands what is to be done. Communication will be as simple and straight-forward as possible. If necessary, statements like, "Now Joan, you tell me what you are going to do with this analysis." should be used. Until work has become established routine and whenever established routine is to be changed, one must be especially careful to be certain instructions are well understood. *DO NOT ASSUME.*

One of the keys to being understood and getting acceptance is *NO SURPRISES*. There is a psychological principle known as "situation set" which describes the fact that persons react emotionally to sudden changes in what they had expected to do. When your spouse suddenly says, "Turn right!" when you had expected to go straight through an intersection, you are upset even though it is a small thing. This same principle applies when you issue an unexpected order or change an established routine. Take the time to prepare the way so the person you are instructing doesn't react badly. In fact a bad psychological reaction can even mean that the person doesn't hear what you have said, or only hears a portion of it. The approach or words to use are just what you would expect. "Mary, we have been working on an improved way to operate our LAN and I think you will find that it makes life easier once you start to use it. Let me go over it with you" or "Tom, I know you were expecting to go to Chicago this afternoon, but we need your help in finishing the Associated proposal. Is it possible to move your appointments back a day and go tomorrow afternoon?" Rather than a blunt, "Tom, I want you to cancel your trip to Chicago." or "Mary, sit down. I want to show you the new LAN procedure." In both cases leading in to a change with an explanation and the opportunity to discuss the matter will make for better management.

When performance is not satisfactory, there is a right way and a wrong way to correct even the simplest situations. Here is an example from a factory situation:

> "John, let me borrow that mop for a moment. I think you would find it much easier to mop the floor using long strokes like this…. Let me see you try it. Good! That's the way—isn't it a lot easier? Just keep it going like that."

> Not: "John, you certainly are stupid! Didn't I tell you that's not the way to mop the floor. Here, watch me. Now don't let me catch you doing it any other way!"

After the second outburst in the presence of the rest of the shop, you can be sure John will do his best to prove you are wrong. In any case he will never forget that you think he is *stupid*.

In a government office the situation might be:

> "Charlie, you seem to be having a good deal of trouble with that 503 Form. If you would set up all the entries and make the calculations on the 503 Grid first, I think you would avoid the problems. Here let me show you."

> NOT: "Charlie, hasn't anyone ever told you about the 503 Grid? You're just being dense to try to do that 503 the way you do it."

Again, correction should be helpful, not a personal attack. When performance is not what you would like, ask yourself, "Am I expecting more from this person than he or she is capable of?" You must also think, "Have I been clear in my instructions? Have I provided the necessary tools or background information?"

In cases where discipline is required, the talk must be as private as the situation allows. If it is not possible to retreat to a private office, at least voices must be kept down and others kept from hearing what is going on, by taking the person aside or otherwise getting out of the middle of things. In the simple case there is no need for elaborate preparation, but the message has to be fair and crystal clear:

> "Mary (or Miss Jones), you know that this office starts work promptly at 9:00 A.M., but I notice you have been late three of the last five mornings. What's the problem?"

After hearing what Mary has to say and assuming you cannot tolerate the behavior, you move on to:

"Well, Mary, I understand what you have said, but the reason we have a fixed starting time is so everyone can depend on the office functioning at that time. In this office we start on time, and I expect *you* to be on time. Now, I'm asking you to do whatever you have to do to be punctual and I expect you will be on time from now on. It's an important part of your job."

On the other hand, if you wish to tolerate a lack of punctuality for some valid, temporary reason, it is important to let others in the workplace know why. This doesn't have to be a big deal, but you must see that the word gets out and that the permission is fair, not favoritism.

"Mary is having a tough time at home just now because her husband is ill and has to have some care in the morning. With my permission she'll be coming in a little late in the mornings until the situation gets straightened out."

If the problem is not temporary, you have to make the choice of changing Mary's hours so everyone knows her hours are different (and the change has to be significant, not just a few minutes!), or getting her out of your department by transfer or termination. It is just this kind of a situation where "temporary" has been allowed to become permanent that is seen as favoritism in the eyes of the other employees. No matter how well intended and how innocent, favoritism is fatal to morale.

A variation of this situation is today's "flexible work arrangements". With more women in the work-force and low levels of unemployment as this is being written, many companies are making special arrangements for employees to work a non-traditional schedule. It is just as important that other employees understand the circumstances of these special arrangements which are more permanent in nature as it is the temporary variations. Once again, what the manager needs to do is to be certain that favoritism has not entered into the arrangement and that it is not seen as favoritism by other employees.

Discipline is not always the answer. Often the same result can be accomplished by emphasizing proper behavior. In Mary's case remarking on the fact that she is *on time* may be as good a way to encourage punctuality as discipline when she is not. The point is that people like to know that you recognize and appreciate good performance as much as you don't tolerate poor performance. Where commendation has been earned, it should be freely given.

In those cases where real discipline is required because of failure to perform on the job, preparation is required. Except in cases of immediate danger such as—"George, take over this reactor. I'm relieving Tony of his duties! Tony, go to my office and wait for me. I'll see you as soon as we get this unit under control." you should take the time in any disciplinary action to write out a few notes and to decide just what action to take, checking it with your own boss if that is necessary. (It is a good rule to follow that no one can fire an immediate subordinate without his own boss' approval.) The emphasis has to be on the job and its requirements and not on personality. Anger also has no place in dealing with people, no matter how provoked you may be. Remember, "Those whom the gods would destroy, they first make angry." If you are still raging about an incident, postpone the meeting. Never act in anger!

Many men have been wrongfully hanged. (A.Conan Doyle, **Adventures of Sherlock Holmes**)

In preparing notes for a disciplinary session, you should answer the questions:

What is wrong or unsatisfactory with this person's performance?

How do I know? Do I really have the facts in the case?

What has to be done to restore satisfactory performance?

Is punishment warranted? If so, what? No idle threats!

You must be in position to, and willing to, administer whatever punishment is in order.

Always remember the person you are disciplining knows very well how his performance stacks up with his fellow employees. If *you* are doing *your* job the employee knows, or should know what is expected of the position he holds and how well he is carrying out the responsibility. He may have made excuses in his own mind to justify his behavior and you should determine what that state of mind is as you get ready to discipline.

When it comes right down to it, in most situations the available options for punishment are few:

Termination.
Reduction of bonus or other incentive compensation.
Withdrawal of promotion or recommendation for promotion.
Assignment to a less desirable job.
In some union situations, penalty lay-off.

Actually, the objective of any discipline is to restore satisfactory performance. It is almost always better to correct the performance of the employee you have, if that is possible, than to take a chance on the person off the street whom you don't know. In other words termination of employment doesn't necessarily solve the problem of poor performance. On the other hand, when the other options are not appropriate or if performance does not come up to expectations after discipline, termination is often the right solution for both employee and employer. You may be doing the person a real favor by getting him or her out of a situation where that person never will succeed.

An interview might go something like this:

> "Henry, I have been disappointed with the performance on your job recently. Specifically, the accuracy of the reports isn't what it was. You must have felt the same way. Is something wrong?"

At this point, *listen!* There may be circumstances of which you were not aware which are affecting the accuracy of Henry's work. If Henry depends on the work product of others, you may have the wrong culprit. On the other hand if Henry basically admits his guilt in whatever fashion, it is time to bore in.

> "You know, Henry, the work of this department is vital and we just can't tolerate errors on that job of yours. What do you think has to be done to eliminate the errors?"

Again, this is your cue to listen. If Henry has the right approach to the problem, your task is much simpler. If Henry has the wrong approach or a hopeless approach, you have to decide right then whether it is worth trying to keep him on the job. If it is, you must coach him on what is to be done and *set a date* for a review of his performance. Be particularly careful to hold to any review date you set or Henry will think you aren't serious.

If the case is hopeless, you may have to say something like:

> "I'm really concerned about your future on this job, Henry. It just doesn't seem to be your cup of tea. Think about it for a couple of days and let me know next Tuesday whether you want to work at improving up to our standards or whether you would rather go back to job X where your performance has always been good."

Obviously, the last exchange could also have been a termination if Henry had been properly warned over a period of time about his substandard performance and warned that termination was a possible outcome of his failure to improve. Remember that "proper warning" in cases of termination or other penalty should *always* include a written record in the personnel file of which the person in question is aware. In that case the following might be the words to use (You should have determined the details of terminal pay etc. ahead of time so you are perfectly sure of your ground):

> "Henry, I am not satisfied with the improvement in the quality of your work in spite of our having talked about the problem before. This week there were three instances when I had to send the daily activity report back because of errors. In spite of your efforts, I can only conclude that this is the wrong spot for you. The last time we talked I told you that if your work did not come up to standard, we would have to let you go. That time has come, Henry, and I want you to plan to leave at the end of the month. In accordance with company policy, you will receive a paid terminal leave of six weeks and you will get your vacation pay. I've made an appointment for you at Personnel on Friday at 2:00 P.M. They will explain about continuing your health insurance and all the other things you need to know. I'm sorry it had to work out like this, but it is better for both of us to face the facts now."

Even in the very small company it is important to take sufficient time with cases of discipline. There may be no formal "personnel record", but you should set up a file into which you put notes of your conversations with the employee and when it comes to termination, there should be a full, written statement of the circumstances and what the termination arrangements were. In this day and age, it is easy for a disgruntled employee to sue or to get a government agency to investigate. You don't want to spend your time defending an action without proper records.

Some managers feel that once an employee has been terminated, that employee should leave immediately. This is a decision that has to be made on a case by case basis depending on the personality of the individual involved. Certainly being let go is a shock and often putting the person on terminal leave immediately is indicated. In small groups or departments it may be wise to get the group together after the individual has left to be certain that the work is being covered and any questions about the circumstances answered. Don't try to gloss over the situation.

This dialogue brings me to the important quality of *intellectual honesty*. People are quick to sense when you don't "level" with them. Nothing destroys the relationship between a boss and his people faster than being "sharp" or "cute" with them. When you deal with people, you must be square and honest. This doesn't mean you have to tell them all you know, but it does mean that what you tell them has to be the straight story. It's like dealing with the press. It's perfectly acceptable to say, "No comment" or "I don't want to or can't talk about that yet." It is *not* acceptable to lie or tell half-truths or embellish stories. Once your people think they can't get the straight story from you, they will in their own minds question everything you say. Telling the truth isn't always easy, but it is the only way.

The people you supervise can also expect you will live up to the same standards you set for them. If the starting time is 8:30 A.M., you should always be on the job at 8:25 or earlier. If the lunch break ends at 1:00 P.M., you should be back by 12:55. If you expect people to work up to the closing hour, you should, too! And you should be consistent in applying rules to everyone. If some are going to be allowed to get ready to leave before quitting time, everyone should be given permission to do so. (This example doesn't mean I approve of having people knock off early to get ready to go home! It's a very tough privilege to handle in a way that doesn't lead to abuse.) These little things count more in the minds of people than the big exception. If you expect your people to work hard and at a sustained pace, then you must do so, too. They will be taking their clues from you. Finally, they will expect you to know your own job and to be doing it in such a way they can be proud of your performance!

Your people have a right to expect you will give them clear direction as to what they are to do and how you want it done. In many cases the latter is determined by time bonus standards or standard procedures, but even in those cases you should make it clear to your people that you want the standards followed. Ask questions to be certain the assignment is understood. There are basically two kinds of work assignments. One is the direct order to do a specific task such as "Mary, will you please fill out the stationery requisition and take it to supply by 10:00." The other is delegation as in "Mary, I would like you to be responsible for our stationery supplies. You will have to check the inventory every week, make out the requisition and bring back the necessary supplies from the stockroom? If you have any problems, be sure I know about them right away." To the extent you can delegate tasks rather than having to give specific orders each time, you free up time for other purposes.

When you get the chance to reinforce good performance by handing out a compliment, do it! It's more productive than discipline. It is always good practice to hand out a compliment when it is earned-and to hand it out so others can hear. PEOPLE BASICALLY WANT TO DO WHAT THE BOSS WANTS THEM TO DO—IF THEY ONLY ARE CLEAR ABOUT WHAT THAT IS! Here are some examples of how good work can be reinforced:

> "Charlie, this analysis is right on the mark and in exactly the form we like to see."

> "Joan, I was happy to see you made bonus yesterday. Keep up the good work."

"Elizabeth, this report is so good I'm going to send it on to Mr. Worley so he can see what good work you do."

"Sam, you did a fine job picking up that arhythmia in Mrs. Jones."

It is in these little daily contacts with your people that you set the tone and build the record which leads to the kind of relationship you have with them. In dealing with people ask plenty of questions and *listen* to the answers. Where there are problems, be sure you understand the circumstances and then follow up to correct whatever is wrong. Often the best thing to do when a problem is posed is to ask your subordinate what he or she thinks should be done. They know more about the details of the job than you do and may well only want confirmation of what they know is the proper solution to the problem. The extent to which you can solicit assistance from your people actually determines what kind of a boss you are and how effective your leadership can be. Every contact should be a training contact. After each interchange, the person with whom you spoke should be taking something away that will improve his or her performance. They *must not* get the feeling that you are too busy to talk with them. It will be interpreted as your not being interested in them and their problems. When you are in a hurry, just make a point of saying something like, "I'm on my way to the Friday Conference. Let me get back to you right after lunch. Will that be O.K.?" Then be sure you do get back to that person. Don't say, "Can't you see I'm busy?" What they have to say could be *very* important.

You also have the responsibility of keeping your people informed about how well the group as whole is doing and what developments may be important to them. "The team won't play to win if they can't see the scoreboard!" Your people will appreciate being kept up-to-date on events so they won't be surprised and so they won't appear to be "dummies" when their friends know and they don't! Depending on the size of the group you may want to make a point on your daily round of getting the news out, or you may wish to have a regular meeting for the purpose. In any case don't forget!

Which brings me to my final point. While there are many exceptions, most of the people you are called on to supervise will spend their entire lives doing essentially the same thing. A librarian will always be a librarian albeit of more senior rank and grade. A guard will always be a guard. A mechanic will always be a mechanic—and so it goes. But, most of them like to feel they can be something more. To the extent you can either offer them the opportunity for training that could lead to advancement, or can make their lives more meaningful by explaining the part they play in the whole, or by letting them in on how things are going in the portion of the business which they comprehend, or by tapping their deep experience, you will improve the productiveness of your organization. No one knows the ins and outs of your unit better than the long-term member. Give them the satisfaction of contributing from their long experience. Once in a while you will find someone who blossoms under the opportunity for instruction or for special assignment and goes on to do more than he or she ever thought possible. Stretch your people! See just how far they can go! Make them all they are capable of being! You will be well repaid for the effort and the occasional disappointment.

NET-NET

That's about all there is to it—sort of "Do unto others as you would have them do unto you", but always consistent and always predictable.

First you have to know your *own* job and *work* at it.

Then you have to be sure that all your people know at all times exactly what is expected of them providing whatever tools or training is necessary.

After that, you must deal "fair and square" with them all: even-handed in administering the rules by which everyone works, quick to reinforce good performance, but equally sure to correct or eliminate unsatisfactory performance, and absolutely honest in all your dealings.

Finally you must bring out the best in your people by making it possible for them to become all they are capable of being and by stretching them to do all they can do.

The satisfaction of knowing you are a good manager is soul-satisfying. By your efforts you can bring out the best in your unit and everyone will share in the accomplishment. Even more, your skill as a manager will be universally admired and that is something that no one can take away from you.

CHAPTER 3

MORE ABOUT PEOPLE AND HOW TO MANAGE THEM

The essence of most business is repetition. Every working day in a manufacturing business materials must be received, product manufactured, orders secured, shipments made, records kept and receivables collected. The same is true in service businesses where the specific elements are repeated over and over—like the motions involved in serving billions of Big Macs or processing thousands of income tax returns! It's also true in non-profit operations like libraries or museums where books have to be given out and catalogued or visitors received in a daily routine. But it isn't only in the institutional world where repetition is the norm. Doctors see patients with similar complaints day after day and one after the other. Judges handle court dockets full of cases that are minor variations of a common theme, and so it goes. To be sure there are a few individuals in society whose activity is not fundamentally repetitious, but these individuals are truly the exceptions.

The fact that life in general and institutional life in particular is repetitive means that most employees do essentially the same thing day after day. In thinking about organizations and in thinking about how to deal with people, it is imperative to give proper weight to this phenomenon. When one gets right down to it there are four, or at the most five, basic categories of employees. Each category is made up of persons called by many different job titles, but all these can be consolidated under just the following classes:

Workers
Technical Specialists
Supervisors or Managers
Innovators
Strategists

WORKERS AND TECHNICAL SPECIALISTS

Just a brief word about these categories before considering the implications. "Workers" and "Technical Specialists" are characterized by the fact that what they work on is what they are told to work on or what they are expected to do in their position and the task is done *right now* i.e. the tasks are immediate and repetitive regardless of level of compensation. A professional basketball player with a million dollar annual salary has to concentrate on *this* free throw not one he might be asked to make two years from now. He has to play to win *this* game, not some future event. The person on the assembly line has to take care of the unit which is immediately at his station. No need to worry about tomorrow's unit, or yesterday's for that matter. Even the concert violinist has to hit the *next* note and can't do much about what is past or what is still to come in the concerto.

The point is that no matter how much training is involved or what the level of compensation, the "worker" or the "technical specialist" is oriented to the assigned task at hand. Once on the job most workers tend to continue doing the same type of work for their entire career. They may become more skillful; they *will* become more senior, and they may do more of, or a somewhat more complicated version of, the original task, but still essentially the same work.

One must consider the "Technical Specialist" as a class of worker since even though the time frame may not be quite so immediate, the work is still task oriented and what has to be done is well-defined. Being a "specialist" requires extra training and a particular orientation, but repetition is still the essential element. The jobs may be very well paid as for instance our professional athlete (who after all is a workman in a type of business), but they repetitively do what they are told (or the coach will have *his* say!) just the same way an office clerk does and, when they are working, do essentially the same thing day after day. In modern society this class of "Technical Specialist" as a "worker" is a very large class indeed. It includes most chemists, most electronic engineers, most computer programmers, most surgeons, most accountants, most librarians, most airplane pilots, most physicians etc. etc. The point is that compensation doesn't differentiate one of the general basic categories from another nor for that matter does the amount of education or the number of college degrees, rather the differentiation comes from the fundamental structure of the jobs and the time span focus inherent in the tasks. Like the "worker" these "technical specialists" do essentially the same thing for their entire career. Active careers may cover different time spans. A professional basketball player has a much shorter active career than an analytic chemist or a physician, but while each of them are active they are a special class of worker essentially focused on the task at hand.

It should be noted that there is a special class of "Technical Specialist" who works by him or herself as a self-employed person. They bridge the categories of specialist and supervisor in that working for themselves, they must do some of the things which a supervisor or a manager does. As we analyze and describe the managerial function, this should be clear.

SUPERVISORS AND MANAGERS

"Supervisors" are the managers of this world and include all those persons regardless of title whose task is directing the efforts of "workers" including the "technical specialists". The essence of a supervisory job is to do as little "work" of the type done by the workers or the specialists as possible while anticipating future events in such a way as to focus, organize and direct the effort of the workers and specialists to optimize for the business or other activity the results of that effort. Supervisors are found in all organizations as the "line officers" of the establishment. Making decisions is a hallmark of the supervisory position. The time pressure on the supervisor is not ordinarily the present moment as it is for the worker, but rather is that of anticipating the next event and deciding what adaptation of resources will be required to keep the activity going as it should. **Supervision is thus the management of change and the practice of human relations coupled with the ability to make decisions.** The supervisor may need nearly as much technical skill as the workers or specialists being supervised in order to understand the significance of events and the actions needed to cope with them, but he or she is not primarily a practitioner of those skills.

Supervisors/ managers are the third most numerous class after workers and technical specialists and like the first two are found at all levels of compensation.

INNOVATORS

"Innovators" are a very small class. They might be called the seminal thinkers of society and their work is *not* repetitive. Being an "innovator" is not a question of the amount of education or of the amount of money at one's disposal, but rather results from a certain mind set combined with a God-given talent which makes possible seeing combinations not apparent to others. Innovators are found in all walks of life from athletics to art to religion to business, but any organization can tolerate very few real innovators (in fact needs only a few) because they upset the routines and because implementing their ideas requires the time and effort of others, often in massive amounts, and implementation may also require money. Both the effort and the money have to be taken from the regular tasks and resources of the institution. It should be apparent that innovation, important as it is, disturbs the essential repetitive patterns of business or other organized activity and thus can be tolerated and absorbed only in small doses!

On the other hand, progress comes from the ideas of innovators. Without them we would all still be living in caves. With a few notable exceptions (Microsoft's Bill Gates for example) innovators are *not* well compensated or rewarded for their work and often are not rewarded or recognized at all until after they are dead and gone. When they work alone as creative composers, artists or inventors, their ideas are often exploited by others. When they work in the structure of a business or other organization, they tend to be viewed as the "resident genius" to be cared for, but kept under wraps. One characteristic of the innovator is that he or she does not work to a timetable. It may be relatively easy to state problems to which solutions are needed or areas for which concepts are required before more progress can be made, but the insight or seminal idea which leads to the new product, to the new enterprise or to the solution to a stated problem chooses its own moment to appear. To be sure such answers are much more likely to occur when one is looking for them and are much more likely to be of value in fields where one has competence and the ability to reduce the idea to practice. Most difficult of all is to predict the timing of the totally new concept for which no need has been defined and which appears so to speak "out of the blue". But analyzing innovation is not the purpose of this book. The manager must simply recognize that he or she may have an innovator to manage!

STRATEGIST

The last category, again a very small class and perhaps of all, the one where consistent good performance is most difficult to achieve, is the "strategist". It is the strategist who must deal with the greatest uncertainties, has the least control of the elements and must look most deeply into the future. The task of the strategist is to assess what is known about a situation and to take positions which optimize opportunities for the institution with which he or she is associated or for her/himself if alone. Like the innovator, there is little that is repetitive about the work of the strategist although in making assessments he or she may be dealing with elements that recur. As in the other categories, there are all degrees of strategists and all levels of compensation. The real top management in a large corporation, and often in other organizations or institutions as well, is made up of two or three strategists along with a "chief decision maker" of whatever title who make the positioning decisions. The top manager may also act as the main "supervisor" of the institution in that he may be called on to make final decisions on certain matters just because the decision is dependent on or sets the strategy to be followed. Successful developers and deal makers are strategists as is the aide to the local politician who decides which issues and what position on the issues will win for the candidate. The President of the United States is or should be essentially a strategist. Strategists are characterized by their ability to think conceptually and by being able to express concepts in concrete terms on which others can take action. They are able to distinguish the relative importance of the factors or elements in any given situation and to see the combination which leads to the prize. More than in most other categories the performance of the strategist improves with experience so long as the person is not so financially successful that he or she stops working. Most good strategists are not much good at anything else including being managers, but as a class their compensation probably averages higher than any other.

This is all very interesting, but what use is it to the reader? First of all, recognizing the characteristics of the various categories allows one to understand more clearly the structure of organizations and why people behave as they do. Secondly, comprehending the nature of the different categories allows one to analyze one's own capacities in looking for a career path with the best chance of success and of job satisfaction. Finally, realizing that for any organization to be successful, there must be a balance among the categories may make the difference between success and failure in the unit where you are employed. The old saying of "Too many chiefs and not enough Indians" is still very much at work!

Since this volume is directed mainly at the "supervisor" or manager category, let's look at how these ideas apply to the job of supervising. Taken in the most philosophical way, the manager's task is to translate the results of the innovator and the strategist into concrete work product by getting the "specialist" and the "worker" to do what is needed. That sounds pretty complicated or theoretical when the group being supervised may be a small department in a large organization. But is it?

As manager you have been given certain resources, personnel and equipment, to work with. Your group has also been given a "mission". That mission grew out of some innovator's idea about a product or a process or some legislative initiative or a concept (maybe for a great museum or a special school) which was taken by a strategist and worked into the institution by which you are employed. You now are in charge of one unit of that institution. Certainly, the first thing you should do as a manager is to have quite clear in your mind just what the mission of your little group is (some people call it function) and how it relates to the whole. This may sound unnecessary when your department consists of five people and it is clear that its "mission" for example is to maintain the accounts receivable or to process incoming gift tax forms. On the other hand, all the activity of your group should be directed to its mission and just taking the time to have clear in *your* mind what that task is, means you have taken the first step in being able to manage. One of the recent approaches to improved performance is the so-called "Team Organization" where the members pool their experience in accomplishing the work of the unit. If this is the culture of your unit, your function becomes more that of the coach than the traditional "boss", but managing such a team still requires a clear sense of mission.

Being a manager is essentially a *state of mind.* You have certain resources in people and equipment to accomplish your "mission". It is up to you to divide the work that must be done into tasks which can be handled by the people you have, or in the team approach to get your team to understand what those tasks are and who can best handle them. You must anticipate events so you can tell people what to do. You must be able to cope with the unexpected which interferes with getting your mission accomplished on time and to an acceptable standard. If your work force is a bunch of sweepers, it may be as simple as being on hand when the shift starts to tell each person in which area to start sweeping. If your work force is a group of financial analysts, you may have had to scope out the whole job yourself in order to decide just which portion should be worked on by Francine and which by Tom and in order to tell them just what it is that requires analysis. The difference in the "state of mind" is that you work from the mission or function of your group and the people who work for you work on the piece of that function which you assign to them or to which they are assigned as a member of the team and under conditions which you specify.

The "Manager's State of Mind" involves the ability and willingness to make decisions. The "Worker" and "the "Specialist" do not make decisions of the managerial type. Both make "choices" as to which of their skills to apply to a particular task, but the decisions about what to do and when to do it are made by the manager based on his or her judgement about what is required to carry out the function or mission of the group or to cope with circumstances which would prevent accomplishing that mission. Said in another way, the manager determines the structure of the task and the worker or specialist provides the skill. It is the latter two who respond to the question about what is going on by saying, "Don't ask me. I just work here." Mind you, in the established unit many of these decisions do not have to be made every day. Given the repetitive nature of jobs, many decisions become standing orders and the division and sequence of work is well known. The decisions that have to be made are those required to manage change and to manage the problems resulting from outside forces that upset the established routine. The manager is "mission oriented", the worker is "task oriented". The manager thinks about the performance of the entire unit without personalities, the worker thinks about "me".

An important aspect of decision making is **Practice makes Perfect**. Many find it difficult to just make decisions and live with the results. The more possibilities one sees in a situation about which a decision must be made, the more alternatives there seem to be, the tougher it is to make the *perfect decision*. For instance, every new President of the United States comes off the campaign trail having made promises about what is going to be done once elected only to find that the "real world" is infinitely more complex than the campaign world. Decisions about actions to take are tough to make. This same phenomenon occurs at any level. The new manager who was critical of the way things were being done by the previous boss finds that maybe those decisions were not so bad after all!

To decide is to act or to authorize action. Bernard Baruch, successful in both business and government, once wrote about making decisions:

"First, one must get the facts about a situation or problem.

Second, one must form a judgement as to what those facts portend.

Third, one must act in time—before it is too late."

It is making decisions *in time* that is the trick and it is this aspect of decision making that is helped most by practice. Once action has been taken on a decision, regret is a waste of time! Not only is it an emotional drain, but it means you are looking back rather than thinking about what is ahead. don't regret a bad decision, just learn from it and make a better one next time.

"Good judgement comes from experience but experience comes from **bad judgement**."

The only thing worse than "regret" is *indecision*. Not only is inde-cision likely to make you miss the proper timing, but it also uses too much mental energy that would better be applied to something more productive. There are, of course, many important decisions where plenty of time is required to be certain that all the facts are available. Decisions on personnel and organization which affect careers and lives are better made deliberately rather than too fast, but for ordinary, day-to-day decisions usually the more quickly the decision is made once the circumstances are known, the better. With practice the man-ager/supervisor can become really proficient. What is required are *excellent* decisions not *perfect* decisions!

This brings us to another quality of a manager, the ability to antici-pate. While the workers in the unit are busy working, the manager has to be thinking about what is coming next. His sources of input for this range all the way from the morning newspaper to the "scuttlebutt" in the lunch room. It is his responsibility to absorb and prepare for impending change so it does not affect the output of the unit. By antic-ipating what is likely to happen, the manager can plan and have deci-sions ready when the time comes and in this way minimize the impact on his people. If some event is likely to mean loss of jobs in his unit, by anticipating he may have time to prepare his people for the bad news so it does not come as such a shock or he may be able to bring in some other work or arrange for transfers before the fact. In any case, anticipation comes from being *aware and alert* to changes or outside events which affect his unit and its people. You can think of plenty of examples, but for instance, learning at lunch that Department A is hav-ing trouble with one of its key processing units may mean that day after tomorrow *your* unit will be short of one of its critical component parts. The time to anticipate what you will do if that proves to be the case is *today!* Or you may learn that in the governor's budget the appropriation for your department has just been cut. The time to start arranging transfers is now!

Finally, one comes to the heart of the manager's job: directing, moti-vating and developing one's people. Into which category does each fit? Does each one really understand what his or her job is? How good is each at what he or she is doing? How fully are his or her talents being used? Where are the problems which affect performance? The manager has to see that today's work is laid out, assigned and done, but the manager also must be thinking ahead to what can go wrong or what can be done to improve performance relative to cost. In the Team concept of organization, the manager may not specifically assign the work to the individual, but the manager acting more as a coach has the responsibility to see that the team is working on the right things and against the proper time schedule. Understanding the mission helps to foresee where problems can come up which can affect the group. It is this thoughtful evaluation of resources against mission which leads to the position descriptions and work plans treated in other chapters. It is also the basis from which the manager communicates the work assignments for worker and specialist alike which get the repetitive job of the group done at an acceptable level of quality and cost remembering that the jobs have to be structured in such a way that they can be done reliably by the personnel available. If the right people are not available, then changes have to be made. Again, this is the manager's responsibility and he or she must make the hard decisions involving his or her people.

How does one go about this task of directing and motivating people given that each of the categories of employee about which we talked earlier has its own needs and aspirations? Let's take the "worker" first. This is the person who basically wants to earn living and have a steady job—probably has no great aspirations to be anything more than the "senior" whatever in order to reach the highest salary classification. Remember however, if the institution has any age whatever, these people have seen bosses come and go and their reaction to your arrival may be, "Here comes another one we have to educate!"

What do you have a right to expect from each of your workers? Dependability, reliability, performance to standard, loyalty, the willingness to follow direction. What do they have the right to expect from you? Respect, competence, orders which can be understood, communication, even-handed, fair treatment, upward representation including getting proper compensation, i.e. standing up for their interests in the organization. When you first take over the job, the employees need very little from you. Unless the whole unit is brand new, they already know the jobs and you would do well to spend your time learning what each does rather than trying to show who is boss. What each person is looking for at first is "respect". Each one needs to establish some kind of rapport with the new boss and the underlying concern is that somehow the new boss represents a threat to job security. You can be most effective at this time by just being friendly and observant, alert to learn more about each person and what his or her capabilities may be. This doesn't mean being overly "buddy-buddy". You *are* the boss and must maintain a little reserve, but it does mean knowing and greeting each person by name, knowing exactly where each fits into the scheme of things and knowing something about the person's background, children, etc. Always keep in mind the old adage, "The further you are down the organization ladder, the more you will be missed when you don't show up for work!"

When the time comes that you must give some direction, each person should expect that your orders about what you want done are clear, concise and in the language of the organization. By that I mean that every organization has its own way of putting things and you should use the words which are familiar to all. If there is any possibility of misunderstanding or if you see the puzzled look, say something like, "Now you tell me just what you are going to do so I'm sure I've been clear about what is needed." Very complex instructions are best written and left with the message, "If there is anything in these instructions that puzzles you, don't hesitate to come back and ask me." Especially in the early stages on a new job, it is important to know that people understand. This is more your responsibility than theirs. After you've worked together for a while, people will know what you mean in most cases.

As you learn more about the way your unit functions, your main responsibility to the "worker" is to improve his competency so the fundamental need for job security is assured. It is your role to see that "Every contact is a training contact", to see that the person's skills are maintained and his or her work meets both performance and quality standards. The way to do this is to reinforce those bits that are excellent or acceptable and to correct by training those that are not. *DAILY*. It only takes a moment to endorse or to correct. "Mary, I was happy to see that you made 20% bonus yesterday." "Joe, that analysis of the Smith proposal was a nice piece of work." or "Sam, let's take a look at yesterday's shipping report. Were you having trouble? Looks like you only loaded 7 trucks. Tell me about it." "Susan, is there something about the new computer procedure you don't understand? The record shows you only booked 500 orders yesterday." Then *LISTEN*. The problem may be something entirely different from what you were expecting.

Everyone doesn't have to be spoken to every day especially when the overall performance is satisfactory, but you must make the rounds of the work stations once or twice every day not only to fulfill your responsibility of assuring competent work, but also to meet the responsibility for communications. If you are not physically present, how can your people hope to talk with you about some problem they may have or anticipate? This can't be done by messages on the computer network or on the bulletin board. It has to be done "in the flesh".

There may be more to being certain your workers maintain skills and competence than what you can do by daily contact. (You may not be as competent as they are in what they are doing!) The money and effort put into properly conceived and structured training programs always pays off. Be alert to chances to get your people into some sort of training program that applies to their work. Where it is permissible and where time allows, do some cross-training on jobs so that a person may be qualified for more than one position. Not only is this motivation for the person involved, but it also helps satisfy that underlying concern about job security. While the responsibility for making the *effort* rests with the employee, it is your responsibility to look for and make available the opportunities to get trained or re-trained.

What about the "Technical Specialist"? This person is usually not nearly so concerned about job security especially if the specialty happens to be in big demand in the market, but he or she *will* be even more concerned about respect and with the chance to maintain competence in the specialty field. The specialist often gets the most job satisfaction out of just practicing his or her specialty and as a manager you may motivate them best by seeing that they are not burdened by a lot of bureaucratic tasks like reports or meetings which they feel just interfere with what they want to do. At very least you must be sympathetic to complaints like, "I have to spend so much time in meetings and filling out forms that I don't have time to work in the lab."

Recognition is a means to show respect, and for the specialist recognition by peers or by higher-ups is worth more than just a word from you. For the worker on the other hand, the fact that the boss knows they are doing a good job means security and that is enough. The Technical Specialist is more concerned about "reputation" and that means that peers and general management must know of his or her accomplishment. As the boss/manager of a unit with technical specialists, you should encourage publication where that is appropriate or you should arrange periodic affairs at which the accomplishments of your technical personnel are recognized. When the opportunity presents itself, let your technical people explain just what is involved in their specialty to the visiting bigshot. If one of them wins an external award, that fact should be made widely known in the organization.

Almost as important is what you can do to help the specialist maintain his or her skill. This is obviously more important in this case than in the case of the worker. You should encourage attendance at local technical societies. If your organization subsidizes additional education, make certain the specialist knows of the programs and again encourage your people to participate. In your "How'm I Doing" sessions try to find out from each person what aspirations they have and help each to identify what steps must be taken to be ready for promotion or for an enhanced career. Your appreciation of their talents and your help in maximizing the application of that talent may well make it possible for your specialists to do and to become more than either of you thought possible.

There is not a whole lot one can do in managing the last two categories of people, the innovator and the strategist. You may or may not have one under your supervision and you may well not need either for the mission of your unit.

With the innovator, the important thing is to recognize the talent. No matter where it shows up, if some person is always coming up with ideas, that person may be an innovator. Managing an innovator starts by being receptive to his or her ideas no matter what you really think of them. By being willing to take and to consider suggestions, you encourage the flow. Perhaps the next idea or the third one down the line will be a winner! The trick is to accept all the ideas, play back those that are not useful in such a way that the next idea will be more useful or practical. If the "idea person" is a worker, it may well be that person should be moved to another department where the talent can be used. It may also be that additional training or education should be arranged. (The same decision to move a person to a new location may be required to maximize the value of the technical specialist.) You will have to make that judgement. The true innovator is likely to be too disruptive to keep in a department whose function is essentially routine, but the talent is so rare it should not be lost to the organization. If you discover an innovator among your employees, talk with your own boss about how best to use that person.

Strategists are in a class by themselves. As individuals, they tend to take care of themselves and there is little you can do if one shows up in your unit beyond providing challenging assignments. So long as the work you have stretches the capabilities of the person, that person will stay. Once the challenge is gone you can expect him or her to move on.

NET—NET

How to summarize the ideas presented in this chapter? Let's go back to the beginning. As a manager you have been given certain resources in personnel and equipment to accomplish the mission of your unit. The equipment is the easy part. It can be defined as to capacity and capability. It is tangible. It can usually be improved by just spending money. About all that is required to keep it functioning properly is adequate maintenance. Personnel on the other hand are none of these things. Almost always people are capable of doing much more than they regularly do and, if properly challenged or trained, able to work at a higher level of capability than that at which they ordinarily work. To get the extra effort requires the understanding of the personality of each individual and the application of the right motivation. This is the same skill a good athletic coach must have. To accomplish the mission of your unit, each person has to be clear about what that mission is, what forces are working to upset or derail the mission and how the individual fits into the whole picture. By making sure that your people know clearly what is expected of each of them, i.e. what part they have to play in the function of your unit, by seeing that each is given the opportunity and the training to become all that they can become and by creating an environment in which every one knows that he or she is respected and will be given a fair deal, you, the manager, have set the conditions so your decisions have a much better chance of being carried out as you intend them to be. Now all that is needed is to be certain that, in spite of all the elements of change and the external forces at work, decisions are made in a timely fashion so the work of your unit is done as it should be today and tomorrow and the day after that. *That is the challenge of the manager.*

CHAPTER 4

HOW TO RUN A MEETING

Let's face it. Meetings have a bad reputation for being a huge waste of time. But you can change all that by following a few simple principles in making *your* meetings effective. There are basically three types of meetings:

The Information Meeting,
The Decision Meeting
The Work Assignment Meeting.

THE INFORMATION MEETING

To begin with let's dispose of the meeting called just to give people some information because that is the easy one. Such a meeting should take the form of "Here is the message." followed by "Any questions?" and "Meeting Adjourned!" This is no time to complicate the occasion by mixing it up with other issues. By that I mean if you want people to concentrate on some particular message don't use the occasion to plan next week's work schedule or to discuss what new system is about to be introduced. The real purpose of using a meeting to get the word out is to be sure that everyone gets the same message at the same time and in the same way, and is particularly valuable for communicating definitive statements or specific policies. All it takes to make efficient use of the time is careful preparation of "the Message" and selection of those to attend. No matter how well you think you know the subject, write it down! And read the specific message you wish to convey. After that you can handle questions off-the-cuff as they come up, but don't try to "wing it" with the message because you are bound to either use the wrong word at the wrong place or to get wrapped up in some side issue. The President of the United States even when making the simplest statement always works from notes and most often from a fully prepared statement. The experts in communications always have their "prepared remarks" before they open up for questions. The statement should be as simple as you can make it and still convey the message. If it turns out there are many questions after you have read the statement, you may not have done a good job in preparing the message. In any case it is a good idea just before dismissing the meeting to go back and repeat once more the written message so the last thing the participants hear is the message you want them to remember. If the message can be easily put on a piece of paper, as for example a new policy statement or a new schedule of some kind, it is always a good idea to give every participant a copy as they leave.

THE DECISION MEETING

The second kind of meeting and one we want to examine in some depth is one called to make some decisions and to decide on a course of action. In this case the First Principle is:

> Limit the meeting to as few people as possible consistent with getting all the facts and include only those persons who have something to contribute to the deliberations.

Before we go further, just a word about committees and where they fit into the scheme of things. In the discussion which is to follow, the word "decision" applies not only to courses of action, but also to strategies. In other words, as well as to decide on some specific course of action, the decision of a meeting may be to adopt a policy or a strategy from which will follow many specific actions. Very often one will find a standing committee charged with making certain types of decisions. In other words instead of having to decide each time who shall be present in a meeting, a fixed membership is established. A good example is a capital appropriations committee which may have the responsibility of screening and recommending to the Board or to the Executive Committee projects requiring capital expenditures above some specified dollar value. Another example is the Acquisitions Committee of a museum or library where knowledge of the details of donations and of collection policy are important. In any continuing committee there is constant pressure to expand the membership. Since it is obviously making important choices, the committee becomes a great place to be "in the know" about future developments that effect people and careers, and membership in the committee carries an aura of being on the inside. Staff personnel particularly covet membership in order to protect their departmental interests. The end result can easily become a cumbersome meeting made up of individuals who really have little to bring to the party. What's more, a secondary effect is that a de facto sub-committee will spring up where the *real* decisions are made. In non-profit organizations "the committee to be on" is often the one most closely related to the purpose of the organization. For example in a museum, it may be the "Collections Committee" or in a social services office it may be the "Case Assignment Committee".

In any case the discussion about meetings which follows applies just as much to the meeting called to decide on the location of the office picnic as it does to the committee which makes major decisions about recommending capital projects or to the committee that decides on assignment of social services cases. **Meetings should be limited in membership to as few people as possible consistent with making good decisions.**

> Second Principle—After limiting the number of persons in a meeting, work to an agenda which has been circulated

prior to the meeting together with pertinent written back-ground material. ***Don't surprise the participants.***

A meeting is no place to read material one has never seen before, or to be confronted with a subject on which one is not up-to-date. The net result is likely to be confusion. The good manager announces the subject of the meeting as far in advance as possible and he sends with the notice and agenda copies of the memos, articles or papers with which he wants participants to be familiar. For example if the meeting is to decide the location of the department Christmas Party, a list of possible places from which the choice is to be made and the probable cost per individual should go with the notice of meeting. The manager also poses in the agenda questions for decision as specifically as he can e.g."Would significant savings be made by dropping product X?" rather than an item like, "Discussion of the future of product X." or "Has the time come to change the location of the Department Picnic?" rather than "Discussion of Department Picnic". With the flexibility of e-mail and computer networks, there is absolutely no excuse for participants in a meeting not having all the necessary background. (In my opinion good decisions cannot be made simply by getting everyone onto the local net. Personal interaction is required to get good decisions.)

In this day of copying machines and e-mail sending out material with the agenda is far more cost effective than expecting each participant to look up in his or her own files the pertinent material. If a meeting must be convened on short notice, it is effective to get everyone together; hand out the material to be considered; and then to specify that the next X minutes will be devoted by the assembled group to studying the material which has been passed out after which the discussion can start. Don't try to run a discussion while some of the participants are reading new material.

When the meeting opens, it is important that everyone knows all the participants. In many, if not most meetings, this is no problem because it is the same old crowd, but if there *is* a new face, don't assume that everyone knows who it is. People clam up in a meeting if they are not sure who is in the group. Welcome participants if necessary, but start the meeting on time. (People soon learn who starts meetings on time and who doesn't. It is a sign that you don't think much of the participants if you waste their time by delaying the start of a meeting.) Being on time also sets the tone for the meeting which is to follow. The opening statement should simply tell what the meeting is all about and what you expect to accomplish. It shouldn't take more than a couple of sentences and it is excellent discipline to write it out in advance. Here are a couple of examples:

> This meeting is to decide whether to close the plant the day after Christmas.

> This meeting is to decide whether to offer ABC Company a discount on its purchases of widgets and if so, how much.

> This meeting is to decide whether to move the location of the Museum Picnic from its traditional site to a new site.

> This meeting is to decide whether we can justify a new copying machine.

No matter how simple the decision to be made, the fewer topics and the more precisely they can be stated, the more effective the meeting.

The next step is to get out of the group the factors needed in making the decision. One good way is to get the group to list and agree on the elements *before* going to any general discussion. This way you can keep the meeting from getting off the track. Here are some words to use:

> Before we make this decision, what do you people think we ought to know? Are there facts we should consider?

Tell me what you people think are the keys to the decision we are facing today.

Well, before we start a discussion, what do you think the important factors are in this case?

You get the idea. If you don't just want a rubber stamp approval on your opinion, you have to get the group talking about the question before you express your own opinion. On the other hand you may need to do some guiding to be sure all the elements you want to get considered do in fact get on the table. This means you should have made up your own list *before* the meeting.

Once the issues have been defined, it is time to get the discussion going. One person is almost certain to be better qualified than the others to state the facts or identify the key elements in a specific issue. Don't let the others smother that person and don't let the discussion get off the mark. If Sally is really the person who is best qualified to speak to an issue, start with her. "What do you think, Sally?" That helps keep the person who doesn't really have a right to speak from taking up the group's time.

Don't you do any more talking than you have to. It may be a good idea to re-state what Sally has said, particularly if you want to emphasize one or another part of her presentation, but your goal at this point is to get the facts and the issues on the table. If you had only wanted to go on your opinion alone, you wouldn't have called the meeting in the first place!

Some people don't know how to stop talking so you may have to stop Joe by saying something like, "That really hits the point, Joe, and now I'd like to ask Charley…" Or you can interrupt by saying, "Let me see if I understand your position, Joe." after which you state his point and then move on to Charley without giving Joe a chance to talk again. You don't want to intimidate people and stop discussion, but this is supposed to be a decision meeting and you need not tolerate the rambler.

When each of the key factors have been evaluated to your satisfaction, nine times out of ten the facts will point rather clearly to the decision. In that case the time has come to terminate the meeting and it's up to you to say, "I guess it is pretty clear from A, B, C and D that the decision has to be…". In other words while you can expect a committee to establish important elements of a decision and to bring out the facts about those elements, you cannot expect a committee to do more than endorse a decision which *you* must make as a result of the deliberations. If this is a "consensus" situation, it is still necessary to state the consensus yourself so there is no misunderstanding of the final position. (You may already have tentatively made the decision before the meeting and merely wanted to re-enforce your position. If no facts have appeared to make you want to change the decision, the meeting will likely result in a better acceptance of what you have decided.)

If you don't want to make a decision on the basis of what you have heard, end the meeting promptly with some words like,"Well you have been very helpful to me and now I have to think about all you have said." or "It seems to me that we have to know more about _____ and I'm asking Susan to find out about X, Y, and Z. As soon as we get that information, we'll get together again." The point is that once you have squeezed all the juice out of this particular meeting, don't let it drag on. Even if *you* don't have anything else to do, the rest of the participants do!

THE WORK ASSIGNMENT MEETING

The work assignment meeting is the one in which tasks are being assigned when it is important for all to know exactly who is responsible for what. This is a combination of the communication and the decision meeting. The "decision" in this case is the job assignment. If the assignments are not routine, i.e. if what each person is to do isn't well understood by all as part of one's regular job, using a meeting for job assignments makes for a smoother flow of work and assures that nothing will drop through the cracks. Such a meeting is an excellent way to develop the details of the best format to execute a program that has been decided on in some other forum. Call together the specific individuals involved in the implementation of the program and pose the questions:

> What steps are required to make this program successful?

> What has to be done by whom and on what timetable to accomplish each step?

Just these two simple questions will bring to light complications or unforeseen consequences which the group sees in the proposed course of action. You will want to probe the complications enough to be certain that what you are proposing to do is still a good idea, then proceed to assignments.

In meetings of this type there may well be more than one topic involved, particularly if this assignment phase is being combined with a typical Decision Meeting. In this case it is important that as each topic is concluded you stop and make clear who has the responsibility for doing what, and when. Don't wait until the end of the meeting although you may want to repeat assignments then. It should be apparent that making the assignments as each topic is concluded clears the air for the participants. By tying up each subject as it is finished, the participants are not tempted to wonder who is going to get which job and thus continue to ruminate on Subject A when Subject B is under consideration.

Each assignment should be written down right at the moment as specifically as possible as to what is to be done, by whom and by what date. If you rate a secretary, this is a good job for that person even though he or she may not be making any contribution to the deliberations. Having the secretary present also makes it possible for you to have that person record ideas or thoughts which come up in the meeting that require further follow-up. In any case it is better to designate someone as the "recorder" so you don't have to do it yourself. Here are examples of assignments:

> "Analysis of overdue accounts assigned to Joe assisted by Sally. Due date 3/1."

> "Meeting with the proprietor of Max's Bar to get detailed specifications for the new patio assigned to Mary to report back to the meeting scheduled for 5/8"

Very often completing a topic and assignment gives one the opportunity of letting "Joe" get back to his job when his part in the proceedings is finished and he has nothing to contribute to other subjects. Unless it is important that everyone know who has been assigned to do what, don't hesitate to dismiss people when their part in the deliberations is completed. The fewer bodies present, the more expeditious the pace of the work. Besides, it is a compliment to people to show you know they have work to do! Be careful not to let the person who is dismissed feel he is being excluded from something he or she has an interest in.

> "Well I guess that concludes everything having to do with the records department so you can go along, Charley."

Having an agenda which clearly shows that none of the remaining topics are of interest to Charley helps him to leave without feeling he is missing something.

Since the work of a committee is done by many minds, it is particularly important that a written record of meetings be made and that assignments be confirmed in writing. The record should concentrate on *how* the decision (or decisions) was made. Such minutes can be very valuable when going back to try to figure out where the reasoning went off the track if a decision proves to be a poor one. One rarely needs to review good decisions, but bad decisions can represent a fine opportunity to learn! You don't have to keep the minutes yourself. A good secretary can summarize a discussion or the task can be assigned to one of the participants.

It is *vital* that assignments be clear and specific as to WHO is to do WHAT and WHEN the job is to be complete. Having minutes distributed helps everyone to have the same story. If there is any confusion at all, it is good practice to have the recorder repeat back each conclusion and each assigned task before the meeting breaks up. Sometimes what the group *thought it decided* and what the recorder wrote down are two *entirely different* things.

Summing up—there are really only three types of meetings although some meetings have elements of all three types.

> The Information Meeting used to communicate to groups where everyone is to hear the same message.

> The Decision Meeting (including meetings to adopt a strategy)

> The Work Assignment Meeting

They all have in common the requirement of selecting the persons to participate, the preparation of an agenda and distribution of background material, starting on time, the need to re-state conclusions at the end of the meeting and to confirm those conclusions for all participants in a written document plus keeping a written record of the deliberations. The better the preparation for a meeting, the more effective it will be. Meetings get their poor reputation mainly because the preparation task is poorly done in many cases, and because the person running the meeting has no clear idea of what he or she is trying to accomplish.

CHAPTER 5

INTERVIEWING

One of the manager's functions is to interview people who want positions in the group. Sooner or later everyone has to do some interviewing. This chapter is about interviewing candidates for a position where one must not only determine technical competence or training, but also try to sense those qualities which make for a good executive or group leader. Interviewing candidates successfully is one of the toughest jobs one has to face and it is surprising how amateurish most people are about conducting an interview. In a period of fifteen to thirty minutes the interviewer must make a judgement about a person that may affect not only *one* career, the person being interviewed, but *the interviewer's* career as well! How to go about it?

To be successful at interviewing one *must* prepare. You must understand well the position for which the person is being interviewed and what is required of a person in that position. Get a position description if one is available (See the chapter on position descriptions). If the interview was scheduled or if the person's resume was received some time ago you should have read the person's resume within the last couple of days so you are familiar with it. Most important of all you should take a couple of minutes to jot down a few things that you **really want to know** about the person being interviewed. More about this later.

The first thing about an interview is that it cannot be done well with constant interruptions. If your office is a zoo with people constantly coming and going, go somewhere else—say into a conference room. If you have a secretary who can stop interruptions for the period of the interview, then stay where you are. In spite of what some people think, one really can't do a good job of interviewing over lunch or over a drink, and trying to interview in the reception area by the telephone operator is a hopeless proposition. I think you get the idea. Interviewing is an important job and should have the attention it deserves.

Just a word about how to interview. Your questions should be the kind that cannot be answered with a "Yes" or "No". They should require the person being interviewed to talk! Realize, of course, that the candidate will try to put the best light on everything so don't put too much faith in the exact answers. The candidate is also likely to try to tell you what he or she thinks you want to hear. One way to get through the veil is to ask questions about past performance. The person has a degree in Library Science. What courses did he or she take? What was the most useful course? The candidate's application shows the person has several patents to his credit. What did the patents cover and how was the work done? You get the idea. Getting the person to tell about his or her own past performance also gives you the opportunity to make some independent checks later. A person is more likely to be at ease when talking about his or her own work experience than on new subjects.

Most important is to let the candidate do the talking! Many interviewers, especially those who are ill-at-ease with the process, do just the opposite. They do all the talking and in effect the candidate becomes the interviewer thus at the end of the session the candidate may have made up his mind about what he or she thinks of the organization, but the interviewer knows little more about the candidate than what the resume shows. There are many techniques to get a person talking, but a simple, "Tell me a little about yourself" is a good one. Certainly it is a familiar topic for the person being interviewed and it allows you to check what the candidate is saying against what is in the resume or application. Another good one is, "How did you come to apply for a position with this group?" As the candidate talks, don't hesitate to make a couple of notes about anything that requires more probing. As the conversation goes on you should be making your evaluation against at least these points:

Is dress appropriate and is the person properly groomed?

Does the person have a high level of physical energy?

Is the person mentally quick?

What has been the performance on previous positions?

How many past positions? Is there a story here?

Too many positions may indicate instability.

If a recent graduate, how well did the person do in school?

Evidence of leadership in school or extra-curricular?

Is the person technically qualified for the position?

What sort of attitude does the person have toward *work*?

Is this person likely to fit the "culture" of this group?

Does this person show the self-confidence required of a manager if managerial responsibilities are involved?

Does the person seem to be decisive and confident?

Let's discuss a few of these points. Certainly, anyone who shows up for as important an occasion as an interview for a job without being properly groomed and dressed is a bad bet regardless of other qualifications. There is little need to elaborate on this point, but the protest inherent in outlandish dress or style is a warning of trouble to come. To be sure, one expects different dress from a research scientist being interviewed in a laboratory from what is expected for an executive at the headquarters in New York City, or an applicant for a factory position as compared to a receptionist in a government office, but there *is* dress appropriate to the position and location and that is what one should be looking for.

Of all attributes, sheer physical energy is high on the list. Work is demanding and whatever the level of the position, physical stamina may make the difference between success and failure. Participation in competitive sport is always a good indicator, but the simple question, "What do you do for exercise and relaxation?" or "What do you do in your spare time?" may tell the story. One can also tell a good deal just by appearance and how the person behaves in the interview. Some people, for example, do not have high energy levels even with the adrenalin of an interview; extreme nervousness may indicate home tensions. Whatever the indicators, be alert since these signs have to be considered no matter how attractive the interviewee may be in other qualifications.

Intellectual quickness ranks right with physical energy as a requirement for success. Does the candidate follow your questions? Does he or she appear alert? Is the job history one where a quick mind was required? One good way to test this attribute is to ask the candidate's opinion about some issue of the day, preferably something related to the candidate's field or the position in question. Try to touch an issue he or she feels strongly about then challenge some element of the response to see whether the person will hold to the point or have good reason for his or her opinion. You don't want someone who is glib, but shallow in thinking.

The best evidence about performance on past positions comes from references. Any candidate should be happy to have you check his or her references. It is worth asking the question, "Is there one of these references that you think is better to check than the others?" Unfortunately, the legal implications of giving references mean that today in many cases about all you will learn is that the person has been employed! Being able to talk with a specific person to whom you may be able to say, "Miss X suggested that I call you to learn more about her performance while in your department. How did she do for you?" is more likely to result in useful comment than a call to the Personnel Department. In any case, you may have to "read between the lines" especially if the person's performance was not satisfactory. One good ploy is to ask, "Would you rehire Miss X?"

At the same time you should investigate the circumstances of frequent job changes if that is what the record shows. There may be a perfectly understandable set of circumstances which was completely out of the applicant's control. On the other hand having had many jobs is often evidence of some basic problem. Don't hesitate to ask for more information if you believe there is something that is not being revealed.

For recent graduates the record at school is another piece of evidence about intellectual power. Your candidate doesn't have to be Phi Beta Kappa, but a good school record is a selective test where the results are already in. Ask about it! It may keep you from hiring a good-looking dolt. Compare what the applicant tells you with what is on the application and ask about any inconsistencies. New technologies and new approaches to even such tasks as being the cashier at a check-out counter demand the ability to understand for which the school record is evidence of past performance. In many positions the school record is part of determining technical competency. If licenses or diplomas are required as part of the technical qualification, don't hesitate to ask for them. Creative people are often asked to bring samples of their work and expect a good interviewer to ask to see them. The interviewer should never feel embarrassed in probing into the skills and background of an applicant. Better to find a problem before the person is hired than six months later!

A more difficult task is for the interviewer to determine attitudes in a brief interview. In the chapter on Career it is pointed out that all organizations are "societies" which from time immemorial in one way or another have ejected members who do not conform. As interviewer, it is up to you to judge whether the person, if hired, can fit into the "tribe". This is a question of attitude and the interviewer has to decide how to test for it. For example, if this organization expects people to work overtime whenever asked, the candidate has to be asked what he or she thinks about overtime. Is the candidate used to working all hours as needed? One has to be careful about certain questions. It is not proper to ask an applicant what he thinks about unions. It is proper, if it is a fact, to say that this is a union shop and all employees must join the union. As an employee, the interviewer knows what attitudes are important to the group and it is up to him to determine where the applicant fits.

After this much background, it is well to talk about the job in question. You should repeat, "The position we are considering you for is _____". Then you can either go on to say something about the position or ask, "What do you understand is involved in this position?" Bring out the bad as well as the good. If the position involves a good deal of travel, say so. If there is shift work, say so. If one is expected to entertain customers at night, say so. If there are periods of intense activity when one is expected to work night and day, say so. You don't want someone you hire to be coming back in a few weeks saying," If anyone had ever told me this job involves _____, I wouldn't have taken it".

Being sure the candidate knows what is involved in the job is important no matter what the job is. DO NOT ASSUME!.

It takes some real effort to describe the downside of a job especially when the applicant may have pre-conceived ideas. One recent trend is the use of video tapes describing what the job is really like. These are expensive and therefore are used only by large organizations like big brokerage houses who must continually fill their ranks of contact brokers. The very fact that turnover is a problem tells a great deal about the difficulty of success on the job. Another example of a tough job is that of the chain restaurant manager where long hours and demanding customers adds to the stress. Here again, the downside must be realistically described to avoid wasting the training involved.

Having explored what the position is all about, it is time to find out if the candidate has some nagging question to which he or she would like to get an answer. Some statement like, "Before we finish, I always like to find out if you have some question to which you really would like to know the answer, but didn't dare ask. Now is the time—anything is fair game. Fire away. I'll try to answer anything I am able to." Following that, if the candidate asks a question you don't want to answer, say so..."That's one question I'm not going to answer because we consider the subject confidential (or `private')". You expect the candidate to be forthright and candid with you and you should be so with them. If the question is one to which you actually don't know the answer, either say so frankly or if it seems important and you are interested in the candidate, take the time to find out what the answer is. If there are no questions, so be it. Don't try to force questions that aren't there.

In ending an interview, you may want to say something like, "Just so you understand, Miss X, my job is to interview as many qualified candidates for this position as I can in the time available and to pick the one who will perform best in this organization. If you are not chosen, don't be upset because that doesn't mean you have failed, it only means that we believe someone else is better suited for this particular position." If you know when the decision is likely to be made, it is good practice to say something like, "We expect to be making our decision by the end of the month and will be letting you know." All candidates should hear one way or the other after a personal interview. Finally, as you terminate the interview, you should always thank the person for his interest in the organization and should see whether there are any courtesies like getting a taxi or being led on to the next interview with which you can help.

Once the interview is over, record your reaction and opinion right away while the whole matter is fresh in your mind. The key question of course is, "Is this a good, solid candidate who would be an asset to and fit into this organization?" That means he or she in your opinion would be able to perform well in the position in question under the circumstances which are normal in the group. A written record is important. It may well be a summary paragraph at the bottom of the notes you took during the interview. Put a date on it and if you are not the one making the decision, report your opinion to whomever you should. If you are interviewing several candidates for the same job, and you should always interview as many qualified persons as possible, it may be helpful to have a kind of spreadsheet or standard evaluation list with the factors you want to assess and on which you can record your opinion of the various candidates. Just put the factors down the side and the names across the top.

One final thought. A person from inside the organization should have preference over an outsider all other things being equal. Not only is promotion from within a sound principle, but one can be much more certain of the qualifications and attitude of an insider who is well known to the organization no matter how carefully the outsider has been checked! Remember the future success of the company and *your* future success depends on the quality of its people. Make your recommendation or your decision count!

CHAPTER 6

JOB DESCRIPTIONS

When you come right down to it, the basic function of a job (or position!) description is to define for *both* the employee and for the boss just what is expected in a position. The usual problem is the description may well be written by a "professional" who uses lots of fancy words, but doesn't grasp the essence of the job. The worst of this lot is the typical recruiter or employment agency whose description is meant to glamorize the job rather than define it. Such a description can easily run five or six pages and be full of such buzzwords as "mission", "parameters", "leadership", "vision", "implementation", "constituencies" and the like. While useful for the purpose of beguiling candidates, such descriptions may do more harm than good if left as the working record. Position or job descriptions have a place in every organization whether for profit or not, whether business or cultural or political. Everyone has the right to know what his job consists of and the criteria against which his or her performance is to be measured.

Writing a good job description takes thought and it takes dialogue between the two persons most interested, the incumbent and the boss. Every good position description has four parts:

Basic function or task to be performed.
Specific responsibilities.

Specific authorities or limits on authority.
Basis for evaluation of performance.

Let's use a couple of examples to make these points clear. Suppose the position is "Assistant to Executive X". The statement about Basic Function might well read:

> "The Assistant to Executive X works with others to see that proposals presented for decision by Executive X are in customary format with facts properly presented and analyzed, and with issues clearly set forth and defined. The Assistant researches and makes frequent reports to Executive X on competitive industry and market trends. As assigned, the Assistant represents Executive X on certain working committees and at industry functions."

It should be clear from that statement that Executive X finds he doesn't have time to wade through the details of capital requests and similar proposals requiring his decision and that he needs someone who can be trusted to check the documents and identify the key issues. (And the assistant may well need to up-grade the quality of the documents being presented by having the time to teach those submitting them to improve their own standards!) Executive X also needs someone on whom he can rely to attend some of the many meetings and public functions where he should be represented, but just doesn't have the time. Finally this person is to read the various industry publications, absorb what can be learned from the public meetings and perhaps do some other field work to keep up on what is happening in the marketplace. It is also clear that the focus of the person on the job is back to his boss. This is *not* the description of a deputy's job. It is not necessary to add "and such other tasks as Executive X may assign". Every job has that extra in it. The point is; a good position description should focus on the essence of the position and not on the elements that are a part of every job. For example, only if it were a unique and vital part of the job would one specify getting to work on time or reading the daily mail!

Moving on to the Specific Responsibilities of our sample job, here are some examples of the way these might be written. There ordinarily should be no more than five or ten Specific Responsibilities:

> "Provides analysis and critical review of proposals submitted for decision. Assists Executive X in arriving at sound decisions on these matters."

> "On assigned tasks, initiates action to see that the work which must be done gets started, makes whatever review is necessary to see that deadlines are met and sees that finished work is in suitable or specified form by instructing others as to acceptable standards and format."

> "Through field observation and continuing comprehensive literature review, develops and maintains a knowledge of "Y" industry with especial emphasis on the commercial strategies of the companies involved. Prepares for Executive X periodic summary reports of industry trends and developments."

> "On assignment, represents Executive X at industry meetings, public functions and in internal committees where a responsible observer is required."

There could be a couple more specific responsibilities, but those four cover the nature of the job pretty well.

Now for a statement of "Authority". This is a tricky situation in this case because the incumbent's authority actually derives from Executive X, but the person is not a Deputy. In many cases, particularly in larger institutions, authorities are spelled out in some Policy Guide and such general corporate or institutional policies control unless limited by one's immediate boss. In this case a statement along the lines of the following is probably sufficient:

> "The person in this position is authorized to take any reasonable and necessary steps to get his work done so long as such action is consistent with established policy and prudent business judgement."

To which might be added in this case a statement that clears the air about the relationship to Executive X.

> "Since in many instances the person in this position will be acting on behalf of and with the authority of Executive X, it is particularly important that the Assistant keep all who should know, including Executive X, advised of significant decisions made or actions taken."

Other cases may require quite specific limitations or definitions of authority. One should be careful about being so specific about authority that the person in the job can't perform if something unusual happens. Position Descriptions and Policy Manuals should only be guides for thinking and should *always* be superseded by good judgement. The only caveat to this rule is that one's boss must be told immediately when actions have been taken that are outside policy limits.

Finally a statement is needed on "Performance Appraisal" so the person understands what he or she is to be measured against.

> "The performance of the Assistant to Executive X will be judged against the following criteria:
>
> The extent to which the person has been able to improve the effectiveness of Executive X by taking the initiative in seeing that proposals requiring decision have been properly worked out, presented in proper format and with issues clearly defined.

The quality and commercial judgement shown in the industry analyses done for Executive X and the timeliness with which the work gets done.

The effectiveness with which the person has been able to work with others in getting acceptance of the strategies and policies established by Executive X and in assuring timely performance against established goals.

The amount of innovative insight which the person is able to bring to the work for which he or she is personally responsible and the skill with which the person communicates at all levels.

The impact of the person's own personal energy and ideas on the performance of the unit as a whole."

Again, these are just examples of the kind of thing one would want to work out in making clear the priorities of the job. It should be clear that these same elements occur in a non-profit institution as much as in one for profit. The trick is to think about the position, to identify its real function and to set out those elements essential to performing the task.

The example below drawn from an actual case involving the manager of a small museum with its associated shop shows how a position description for a line manager might look.

POSITION DESCRIPTION
MANAGER PLYMOUTH FACILITY
Old Dartmouth Historical Society

BASIC FUNCTION

Reporting to the Director of the New Bedford Whaling Museum, the person in this job is responsible for the management, operation and maintenance of the Plymouth Facility within the policies and guidelines laid down by the Director and the Trustees.

SPECIFIC RESPONSIBILITIES

1. Recruits, hires, and supervises both paid and unpaid aides specifying their duties as appropriate.
2. Sees that the conditions of the lease are complied with.
3. Deals with the public and with Town authorities as required.
4. Accounts for and safeguards monies received from admissions and from sales in the museum store in the manner specified by and satisfactory to the Senior Administrative Manager of the Whaling Museum.
5. Arranges with appropriate personnel at the Whaling Museum or with outside suppliers for the supply of articles to be sold in the museum store.
6. Arranges for the maintenance of the physical plant and of the exhibits; dealing with the Landlord, outside tradesmen or Whaling Museum personnel as appropriate.
7. Sees that proper security measures are in place to protect the facility and its exhibits at all times and responds to incidents as they may occur 24 hours a day, seven days a week.
8. Performs such other tasks as the Director may from time to time assign.

AUTHORITIES

Within approved budgets, the person in this position is authorized to take any reasonable and necessary steps required to carry out the responsibilities of the position so long as such action shows prudent business judgement and is consistent with policies and guidelines set forth by the Director of the Whaling Museum.

EVALUATION OF PERFORMANCE

The performance of the person on this job will be judged against the following criteria:

The quality and performance of the persons selected as aides.

The skill with which the relationship with the landlord is handled.

The response of the public.

The condition of the facility and of its exhibits.

The selection, display and acceptance by the public of articles sold in the museum store.

The care with which records are kept, monies handled and budgets adhered to.

The nature of the relationship with the staff at the Whaling Museum.

The impact of the person's own personal energy and ideas on the success of the unit as a whole.

January 1991

Developing a job description for a job which already exists and has been filled is best done by having both the incumbent and the boss write up drafts of the description after which the two versions can be reconciled. Where a job has been done by the same person for a while, the actual job content may be quite different from what the boss thinks it is. While it is the boss' prerogative to set priorities and to specify what is going to be done, it is the responsibility of the subordinate to make his boss aware of what was being done in the job and what needs to be done as he sees it so some important function doesn't get eliminated through misunderstanding.

If you are the new boss (See Chapter 1), you have to find out what people have been doing and a written job description along the lines described above is a good way to do it. You may have different ideas as to how you want the position handled and a job description is a good way to reach a meeting of the minds without losing some vital element of which you were not aware. Likewise as a new subordinate, developing a job description may keep you from doing things the boss doesn't want and doesn't expect you to do. Having job or position descriptions for everyone reporting to you makes a good starting point for the "How'm I Doing" talk which is the subject of a separate chapter in this book.

So far in this discussion, I have used the example of typical, salaried jobs. The principles obviously apply to any position, but it is important to keep in mind the difference between a job *manual* and a job *description.* For example the description for a typical hourly position may be something as follows:

BASIC FUNCTION

The person in this position determines the quality level of parts coming off line B by checking each part to statistical standards using methods and tools set out in the Line B Inspection Manual.

SPECIFIC RESPONSIBILITIES

Understand and make use of all measuring devices used for Line B inspection.

Follow INSPECTION MANUAL procedures to determine whether finished parts meet specifications.

Maintain accurate, legible records of all parts inspected in standard inspection report format.

Consistently work with acceptable degree of accuracy as determined by check inspections and at Line B normal speed or better as set forth in the TIME BONUS MANUAL.

PERFORMANCE APPRAISAL

Performance will be measured by the degree to which the person in this position has been able to maintain a consistent record of error-free inspections while maintaining a normal or above normal output combined with on-time, reliable attendance and the ability to work in harmony with other members of the department.

The details of exactly how to check a widget to specification belong in an inspection manual, not a job description. Time Bonus descriptions of jobs may be an aid to getting the proper elements into a job description, but Time Bonus standards belong in their own volume not in the description itself. Where specified by law or where it really is a requirement of the job, the position description may include in "Basic Function" or in a separate "Qualifications" category some statement such as, "The person in this position must hold a stationary engineer's license" or "The person in this position must have a current teacher's certificate."

In spite of the fact that job descriptions have been used and abused, they are still one of the most valuable of management tools when properly constructed. The trick is to avoid a job description that was written to polish egos or to meet someone's stereotyped manual. To be optimally effective, a job description has to be carefully worked out by the boss with the person involved in language which they both understand. Its main function is to let both know what the real purpose/function of the job is, and then to spell out the specific responsibilities and the basis for evaluating performance in *plain English!* The manager uses the description as he or she thinks about evaluating performance and as a check on whether work in the entire unit has been organized to use the talents of available personnel most effectively. Most of all a proper description ensures that boss and employee are on the same wave length about what is expected and how performance is to be measured.

CHAPTER 7

WORK PLANS

When a business or institution is small, most managers have specific knowledge of what is going on, and the need for action on particular parts of the business or institutional affairs is easy to identify and widely understood. Each person involved can see rather clearly the results of his individual effort, and interaction of the various parts of the operation are easy to isolate. Under these conditions people are usually willing to go ahead and do things on their own since each individual feels very much a part of the enterprise and quite sure of accepted policy. In larger activities it is less clear how everything interacts and what results come from taking an initiative. In fact "the system" in large organizations like public schools or government offices usually makes it "safer" to let someone else make the decisions and take any initiatives for change while you just "do your job". How many times that phrase shows up, "I'm just doing my job". It's a pretty unsatisfactory state of affairs for the thinking person. Doing what one always does, but perhaps doing it a little better as the experience base grows, just isn't enough to make for a satisfying job experience.

One good way of breaking out of the routine and getting the initiative is to have a work plan to talk over with your boss. You will remember that drawing up a list of goals was one of the recommended early tasks for a person taking over a new position. The work plan is another way to do the same thing.

There is no substitute for periodically thinking through and getting down on a piece of paper specific targets for improvement against which to work. It is just too easy to get swept up in the daily tasks with all the time pressures associated with them and think one is being very productive only to find six months later that nothing very significant has been accomplished and it is just the same old grind! It's too easy and it is deadly!

The process of generating a work plan that has some meaning requires some real thought and effort. Ask yourself, "Where can **I do something that will make a difference in this institution?**" Where are the "pressure points"? Which elements account for the big dollars? Is it material cost? Then reducing spoilage, increasing yields, or cutting raw material costs can make a real difference. Is it hours spent on complicated reports? Then rationalization or restructuring may be the answer. Is it sales expense? Then an incentive plan to increase the effectiveness of the individual salesman may be the answer. Is it cash availability? Then a drive to reduce overdue accounts or inventories is in order. In the case of a non-profit it might be that attendance is dropping off and a series of lectures or special exhibits may be indicated. In any case the first step is to determine which elements involve significant dollar values or have a "life or death" quality about them for the institution in which you work. As you think about your unit and where it fits in the total scheme, write down *three or four* specific points as the ones on which you want to work. Don't try to take on too much. These goals are to be over and beyond your regular routine.

The second step is to quantify goals in order to see where the effort should be applied. What is the dollar effect of reasonable or attainable goals. Perhaps all projects cannot be expressed in dollars and cents, but there is nothing quite so effective in evaluating the relative priority as having even rough dollar values assigned to each proposal. For example, if it is *hours* your project will save, you can assume an average hourly rate including fringes to calculate dollars. If nothing else, it helps to take the emotion out of the exercise. At this point it is a good idea to check with your boss to see what *that person's* goals or plans may be for the period ahead. You may even find that something you had planned to work on will be eliminated as a result of a change in strategy or an action which has already been decided on. Some other aspect of the operation may be of more importance in your boss's thinking than you had imagined. Not only does consulting clear the air, but you need your boss's endorsement on any plan you come up with so you will have the authority to proceed. The very act of talking it over will give you new insight into how the operation works and will improve your relationship with the boss.

Finally convert the whole thing into specific action steps with dates for accomplishment. What you should be looking for is what I call "second derivative" actions. Not just "increase yield on product X by 2%", but rather "increase yield on product X by 2-3% from 92% average to 94-95% average by installing new temperature control on base mixer. Completion date: April 5th". Of little use are general phrases like "Increase sales" or "Increase yields" or "Maximize attendance".

Rather than "Increase sales" or even "Increase sales by 10%", try "Increase sales 8-10% from X amount to Y amount by offering new price schedule for larger orders" or "Increase sales by 8-10% by opening southeastern market through manufacturers' representatives"— again with a specific "Complete By" date.

For a non-profit organization it might be something like "Increase applications for admission by 10% from 1200 to 1320 minimum by developing new direct mailing piece by May 1st". For a large government office it might be "Reduce errors in Report 873 by redesigning Schedule B. Completion April 15th". The point is that a Work Plan which simply repeats the broad general goals a person should be working for anyway is of little use. What you want are some specific targets expressed in absolute terms which you can look back on at a review date and *know* whether the job has been done or not. It's best to space out the target dates over the period so work is accomplished in stages. By that I mean that a single goal may involve several steps which must be done in sequence. In that case set target dates for phase 1, phase 2, etc. and specify as precisely as possible what is to be done at each step. Suppose your project is to have plans completed for a new library wing by September 15th. The first phase might be, "Working with the architect determine rough lay-out by March 25th". The second phase might be, "Have preliminary drawings for building permit by May 1st". Then "Secure building permit and all necessary official permissions by June 15th". You get the idea. The basic project will not be complete on time unless the pieces are done properly.

Once established, targets should not be changed either to increase or decrease until the next period when work plans are drawn up. Much can be learned by thinking about what happened when goals prove to be wrong either on the high side or on the low side, or why some specific task didn't come to fruition. Do in-depth thinking about the reasons for failure. What is the "second-derivative"? If the failure was in increasing attendance at the museum, analyze the attendance pattern compared to what you had thought possible and to prior periods for clues as to what went wrong. If the failure was in increased production, what do the actual records show about why the failure occurred. It is not enough to simply accept the results. Perhaps the most enlightening insight comes from *exceeding* a target. Analyzing this deviation may be the key to a breakthrough success. It is easy to just accept success without looking into the reasons when knowing what really happened may set a whole new approach. Where possible, incentive plans should be tied to the goal-setting process. (There is more about this in the chapter on Compensation.) However, work plans are not meant to be incentive plans. The purpose of the work plan is to pull the participant out of the routine and to get some specific results which otherwise might not have been accomplished during the period.

Work Plans are not meant to address the usual tasks of a position. They are meant to give priority to a few extraordinary projects that could make a real difference in the operation. For your own effectiveness, don't try to get too many items. Completing two or three important tasks a quarter in addition to just doing your regular job will soon add up to a significant and recognizable accomplishment, something your boss will notice!

Once you have mastered the technique, try it with some of the people reporting to you. It will add some spice to their jobs and you might be surprised how much it will do for the morale of your unit when your people find out you think they are capable of being innovative. This approach may be particularly useful in fields like education, health care or government offices where procedures tend to become fixed and competitive pressures seem far away. The work plan is a very useful tool of management at every level.

CHAPTER 8

THE HOW'M I DOING TALK

Every person has a right to know what the boss thinks of him. This chapter outlines a way to talk with people whom you supervise so both of you understand each other. Supervisors are appraising people with whom they work all the time. Every time a job is assigned or work is evaluated, every time a promotion is made or someone has to be reprimanded, every time even a casual conversation takes place, you are making an appraisal and something of your attitude toward the person involved shows in your manner. Unfortunately these non-structured exchanges do not fulfill your obligation to see that each person is brought to his or her highest level of capability. If you are sincerely interested in the people who work for you, at least once a year and perhaps more frequently you should have a thoughtful "How'm I Doing" talk with each person who works directly for you *including* your secretary or personal assistant if you have one!

What do you want to accomplish in this conversation?

Let people know where they stand. If people have to guess how they are doing in their work, they are likely to worry when they shouldn't or, they may have a confidence that isn't deserved. No news is supposed to be good news, but we have all seen cases where the boss let a bad situation go

on for years until some event causes a crack-down then
the word goes around, "They were never told and that's
not fair!"

Help people improve. Most people want to do good work and most
people respond to honest criticism which will improve their performance. Often you may think you have told a person what you want
changed, but the message hasn't gotten through for whatever reason.
A thoughtful discussion about a person's goals and ambitions may
lead to much improved performance.

Let people get things off their chest. Strong feelings build up in the
workplace and often are hidden until it's too late to prevent trouble. If
you can get these feelings out into the open *before* the situation
explodes, you may increase the effectiveness of the entire team.

Develop mutual trust and understanding. The pressure of the day-
to-day job often results in our not really knowing or appreciating the
people with whom we work. To the extent you get to know your people and especially know how they feel about their jobs, about their
relationship with others, about their ambitions and hopes, how they
feel about *you*—you can do a much better job of making them as effective as possible. Many of the problems that come up in the workplace
result from misunderstandings on both sides. This is a two-way street
and *mutual* trust is the key.

This sounds great. So why don't all supervisors have "How'm I
Doing" talks with their people? Most will tell you that they already
keep their people informed by talking to them every day. The trouble
is that the kind of thing one does on a day-to-day basis isn't enough.
You may praise someone for a good job as it's done, or criticize for
poor work when it appears (and you should) but that doesn't pull all
aspects of the job together in perspective and give the other person a
chance to say what's on his or her mind. An "open door" is not
enough. People need encouragement to come in and talk. Unless you
are in the listening mood, it just doesn't happen. Besides you're busy!

More than likely the real reason why more supervisors don't have this kind of session with their people is they are afraid to. They think the session will be unpleasant or that it will get out of control. They feel that somehow the whole thing will get off the track and the relationship will be worse rather than better. Actually the task is easier than you might expect. In any case you have a responsibility to your people as their boss and just because it may be tough is no excuse not to do it.

HOW TO GO ABOUT THE "HOW'M I DOING" INTERVIEW

Getting the most out of this process is going to take some preparation. First of all you have to schedule some time when you will have at least half an hour free of interruptions which also works into the schedule of the person with whom you are going to talk. (Don't, for example, schedule the interview so that your person misses the car pool just because you regularly work a little late and it doesn't matter to you.) Let the person know what you have in mind as you set up the appointment. If this is the first time, take a few moments to explain what the interview is all about. The person may not believe you until he has actually gone through the experience, but you should say something like:

> "We see each other nearly every day, but usually are so busy we don't have time to talk so I've started a program of taking some time out now and then to sit down and talk one at a time with the people in our department about their jobs and how things are going. I thought we could talk about what you think about your job, any problems or ideas you may have and anything you want to bring up. Just one rule—this is not a time to talk about compensation. I just want to talk about our relationship and the job in a person-to-person way. So I'll see you tomorrow at 10, O.K.?"

Before the meeting you must think about what you are going to discuss. What things does this person do well? List them. What things are you unhappy about? Jot those down, too. What three or four important aspects of the job make the difference between just so-so performance and super performance? Where is this person likely to be five years from now? Is there some training which would be valuable? Are there things this person does or doesn't do that bother you? If this is not the first talk, review your notes from earlier discussions. This will be an important occasion and it warrants proper preparation. A word of caution, if this is the first talk, "Rome was not built in a day" and you don't have to cover everything in one session. Just pick out three or four important points and concentrate on those.

Have the interview in a comfortable and private place. If your office doesn't provide a place where no one else can hear the conversation and where the two of you can't be seen from outside, then find an appropriate place like a conference room or another office. Don't start the interview unless there is a reasonable chance of finishing it and don't start if you are hurried, angry, worried about some other situation or otherwise not in a friendly and helpful mood. This talk is very important to the employee and deserves every chance of being a success.

At the start of the interview you obviously want to put the other person at ease and make them comfortable. This can be tough especially if this is the first time for the person involved. There are several things you can do to make it go well. If possible, get out from behind your desk into a less formal seating arrangement, but still in a way that you can use your notes without embarrassment. Be yourself! Don't try to be overly friendly. Your people are much more conscious of the gap between employee and boss than you are. It helps to start off with some common incident that is easy to talk about: "What do you think about that new model, the green and gold one that's in the lobby?" or "I understand that bowling team of yours is way out in front. Who's the big star?" or "Did you hear we landed that big order with Standard?"

As soon as everyone is relaxed a little, you should repeat the purpose of the conversation. Your tone should be one of the friend and counselor. You are trying to be helpful.

> "Joe, I've asked you in for this little talk because we just don't get the time out on the floor to talk about you and me and the job. As I told you, this is not the time to talk about salary. I'll be glad to do that at some other time, but today we should just talk about how you are doing and exchange views about how the job is going.
>
> Let me start off by saying that I certainly like the new layout of your work area. That took some thought to work out, but you certainly must feel it was worth the effort. Tell me, how did you get the idea?"

Listen to what he has to say. The idea of ending with a question after the favorable remark is to get him started talking. Listening is half the battle. You are not learning anything when you are talking yet most supervisors find it easier to talk than to listen especially if the person being interviewed is not very vocal. People feel better about someone who listens than about someone who can't stop talking! But you do have to move on to the meat of the interview. Start off with a strong point:

> "Joe, there are some things you do well and some things that you don't do so well. I like the way you are always on time and I like the way you work right up to the bell. Your buddies always look to you when a tough job comes up and you are good at figuring out how to do it...
>
> It does bother me, though, that your 873 Form never seems to be just right. What is there about the way that form is laid out that is a problem?"

You've told him some good things and then brought up a problem. People like to know that you recognize things they do well as well as things they don't do so well. Note also that the question is not one that can be answered "yes" or "no". Use questions that begin with Who? Why? What? Where? or When? and are open-ended. Avoid questions or comments that force certain answers. You are not looking for a "Yes man", but rather looking for how the person really feels. Encourage the employee to explain further when there seems to be a problem. "Go ahead; tell me about it." Listen without interrupting. Nod and encourage—"Mm-hm", "I see".

You want to work from your notes about the person and about the requirements of the job. The idea is not so much an "evaluation" as that term is frequently used when talking about a person and a job, but rather to counsel and be helpful to the employee. You talk about the strong points in order to reinforce these strengths and talk about the unsatisfactory work or attitude in order to help solve the problem. When a problem has been identified, don't simply preach but rather ask the employee, "What do *you* think can be done about this?" Talking about a person's faults is the hard part! Most supervisors dread this part of the interview, but here is where you can really do something to help the person. In most cases you should avoid critical words like *fault, mistakes, shortcomings, weakness* but rather should talk about things that can be *done better*. What you are looking for is *improvement* not a recital of past errors.

Be sure to use examples when you need to criticize and make them recent happenings not something out of the distant past that will make the employee think you are holding a grudge. Avoid comparisons with other people. By asking questions like, "Where do you think you can make the biggest improvement in your work?" or "What can I do to help you do a better job?" you may be surprised to learn that the employee is his own most severe critic.

You can learn a lot by asking, "What do I do that you don't like or that bothers you?" As mentioned earlier, this is an important part of the dialogue. Many, if not most, employees are reluctant to criticize their boss in *any* way. Any indications you get from this or other parts of the conversation about some action of yours that bothers the employee should be developed very carefully. Perhaps the employee says something like, "Sometimes you assume I know more than I do." which can be your clue to return to the subject a little later with, "A little earlier you mentioned that I sometimes assumed you know more than you do. Could you give me an example so I'm sure I know what you mean?" It is up to you to be alert to the little nuances in the conversation. You may not get much feed-back the first time you have a "How'm I Doing Talk", but just let some employee get a message through to you that results in your dropping some annoying habit or results in your changing some practice that is bothering everyone and the word will be around your unit in a flash! Subsequent talks will be more productive.

That brings me to the point of just how frank to be in the interview. Again "Rome was not built in a day." and you should not expect to make a complete reform in one interview. There is a great deal of judgement involved. It is a question of knowing your people. With one person you can be brutally frank and with another you must be extremely tactful. Part of this is dependent on the way you normally communicate with the person. With a friend whom you have known for years you may be able to speak more frankly than with a person who has been around for only a short time especially if that person may be harboring some resentment against you for whatever reason. Ask yourself, "Will this person accept and use what I am about to say on this subject?" If the answer is,"No" then you probably will want to drop the subject. When you don't feel right about discussing some topic, don't do it. Your instincts are usually right. Women tend to be more sensitive than men in taking "personally" criticism which you intend to be helpful.

On one subject there should be no compromise. If during your discussion about the person's hope for the future, you find that the person expects a promotion or expects to have a position that for whatever valid reason just isn't going to happen; you must tell them the truth even when it hurts. You don't want to discourage someone need-lessly, but having expressed the expectation, if you allow the interview to close allowing those false hopes to stand, the person will believe that you have agreed with them. Just saying nothing will be taken as agreement! This is *very* important and difficult as it may be, must be faced and handled.

The person doesn't have to agree with your remarks. You are not trying to get someone to "knuckle under" or "confess". Even when an employee doesn't agree or believes he has been misjudged, there is value in the interview. It is the employee's responsibility after all to prove that your opinion is in error. By telling him or her, you give them the opportunity to prove you are wrong by the way they per-form in the future. You do have to walk a thin line between promises and discouragement. Be cautious about telling people their goals are impossible and don't discourage any serious effort to improve even if you don't think the effort will last or succeed. On the other hand, don't make promises about the future especially about anything that is not completely under your control. If you are not the one who can make good on a promise, the effect on the person of failure to deliver may be disastrous because, relying on your promise, they may have told others or made commitments. Keep your statements simple and direct. Remember people are likely to read into your words more than you may have intended. If there is any question in your mind as to whether what you have said has been properly understood, don't hes-itate to go back over the subject again asking enough questions so there can be no misunderstanding.

It is especially important that you don't dominate the interview to the point that you don't find out how the employee feels about you and the way you do things. You may have some habit or mannerism that cuts into your effectiveness with others. There may be misunder-standings about why you do things the way you do. In any case this is an opportunity to learn. Don't judge the success of the interview by how much you have gotten off your mind, but rather by how much you have learned from the employee and especially by the employee's attitude at the end of the interview. You should close on a friendly note assuring the employee that you are always glad to talk with him or her about the job. If it is true, it is always good to say that you like working with the person.

After the interview, clean up your notes and put them away in a confidential file where others will not see them. They should never be considered the "official" record or you will destroy the tone of the "How'm I Doing" talk. The notes should be for your use only and especially for the next time you have a "How'm I Doing" session. Make a special effort to be aware of the employee's behavior and to compliment them on any positive changes that may be resulting from the talk. If you made any commitments, be sure to follow up on them and if you have had some later thoughts on training or whatever that might be helpful, mention them to the employee. It is up to you to carry on the dialogue which has been started.

There are some special cases that require comment:

> The Veteran—The person who has been with the organization for many years (tenured or de facto tenured) often has special concerns and problems. Don't assume that just because a person has been around for a long time there is nothing bothering him or her. Many people reach a plateau in their careers, but it is a mistake to assume that they are not interested in promotion or transfer. They may also be concerned about their status as younger people pass them up. Changing work methods may make them feel inferior especially in this time of electronic revolution which often applies particularly to the kind of position in which the long-service employee is found. It is just these people on whom you may be depending as the stable core of a department who feel the least secure and are most in need of sympathetic coaching. When changes are to be made in routines, they are likely to be the ones most upset by the new procedures and ready to declaim all the reasons why the

new won't work! You can be particularly helpful if the person is thinking about retirement by making certain he or she gets all the help needed to make a smooth transition. This is a worrisome time for many people. The "Veteran" may also be the one most affected by failure in earlier years to have had "How'm I Doing" counseling. He or she may believe they are doing just fine as a result of the deference shown to seniority and the difficulty, especially for a person with less service, of talking about shortcomings. Certainly with this person having all the facts before criticizing is important. You may very well have to "live with" the long-service employee and should tailor your remarks accordingly.

The Hot Shot—It is usually easy to talk with the outstanding performer, but the job doesn't end there. The greater the ability, the more your responsibility both to the employee and to the company to push him or her along as fast as prudent. There is always the temptation to keep the producer in your own department so your performance will look good. There is also the thought that this person may be so good he or she will take *your* job. (Usually one finds rather that the supervisor who keeps producing and pushing along outstanding people gets pushed along as well!) In any case the interview with the outstanding employee has to center around what can be done to see that his or her abilities are used to the best advantage of both the person and the institution.

Repeated Talks with the Satisfactory Person—You may wonder why it is necessary to have periodic talks with the person who is doing the job well and where nothing seems to have changed since the last talk. Remember what seems pretty routine to you may not seem so to the employee. Don't take it for granted that everything is just the way it was a year ago. What you may learn in your interview may be doubly important just because you think nothing has changed. It is also important that you tell the employee you appreciate the fact that you depend on them. Something like,"I want you to know how much I appreciate the good work you have been doing. The department depends on you." "If everyone were as reliable and careful as you, my problems would be simple. I hope we can keep working together for a long time to come". The interview may be brief, but it is *important*.It is particularly important for the secretary or assistant with whom you are in daily contact. It is *so* easy to believe that the person already knows how you feel about him or her or that you are *certain* there is no problem in the relationship when in fact problems exist.

The So-So Employee—This is the person who isn't bad enough to fire, but who is clearly not entirely satisfactory. The key here is to get to the problem. Once the employee understands that there are parts of his performance with which you are unhappy, there may be a simple answer. Often no one has told the employee and he or she thinks his work *is* perfectly satisfactory. One of the great advantages of this kind of talk is the chance for *mutual* understanding. And understanding comes when *you* listen! Sometimes an employee like this just won't talk. It may be that being unable to communicate is at the heart of the problem. It is up to you to find a subject the person can talk about even though not related to the interview and then once the conversation has started, to steer the talk around to problems. Sometimes it is necessary to have a couple of sessions before the employee can talk freely. It is in this "So-so" category where one often finds the veteran employee discussed above. It is your responsibility to make certain that "so-so" doesn't become "unsatisfactory". If you allow the long term employee to become unsatisfactory, you will be wasting a life-time of experience. Often it is just a matter of re-establishing the person's focus.

The Failing Employee—Most people hate to face into an unpleasant situation. Often the supervisor's reluctance is based on the belief that it will come as a great surprise to the person being told. Actually, it is usually the case that the employee is well aware of the fact that his performance is not up-to-snuff and is relieved when the subject comes out into the open. Sometimes after the introductory words, all the supervisor needs to say is, "Charlie, I notice you haven't been too happy in your work lately. What seems to be the problem?" Get the person talking. Don't try to solve things but rather help the person to see some acceptable solution. You seldom do a person a favor by keeping him or her on a job they can't handle, and you certainly do that person no favor by not heading into a problem of drugs or alcohol. If personal problems like the latter are the cause for poor performance, see that the person gets professional help. If the problem is lack of capacity, you may be doing the person a great favor by getting him or her into another organization or another department where for whatever reason the situation is one the employee can handle before failure means loss of job.

As a supervisor, you have great influence on the lives of the people you supervise. The "How'm I Doing" talk is a powerful tool for using that influence. Just remember, the more effective your people are, the more effective *and successful* you will be.

CHAPTER 9

THINKING ABOUT COMPENSATION

To most employees his or her boss is considered the key to better pay or other forms of compensation. Any manager has to understand about "compensation", how to think about it, how to use it and how to talk about it. This chapter addresses that subject.

Everyone is interested in compensation or at least they say they are. In fact most people don't work for monetary compensation per se. They work for other reasons: because they want to prove something to someone, because society really doesn't tolerate a person who doesn't work during the so-called "working years", because they enjoy exercising their talents, etc. etc. On the other hand monetary compensation is one way to tell how well one is doing in realizing the goal for which he or she is working. It's like the score in a basketball game or grades in school. So regardless of the underlying reason for working, monetary compensation is important—besides it pays the rent!

Because there are so many different reasons why people work, there are also many kinds of compensation, not all of them monetary although most with the clear exception of titles or praise can usually be expressed in dollars and cents. It is important for a good executive/manager to understand the complexities of compensation and to use this understanding in dealing with people. The principles apply to any organization, profit or non-profit where people are paid for what they do.

There are at least five basic kinds of compensation although they masquerade under many different names and compensation consultants make a profession out of running variations on these fundamental elements. The differences are important because a proper mix not only acts as an incentive for performance, but also keeps some other organization from stealing your good people. They are:

>Base or straight dollar compensation paid currently and subject to immediate tax as income.

>Protective Compensation or fringe benefits such as health insurance, accident insurance, vacations, etc. whose impact or application is current. This group is characterized by being relatively easy to express in dollars and cents. Given an appropriate amount of straight dollar income, the individual could purchase equivalent benefits for himself. Converting to dollars is not a simple calculation because the tax consequences to the individual of the various programs are inconsistent and likely to be complicated, but it can be done.

>Perquisites are a form of compensation which combines psychic benefit with a monetary benefit. "Perks" are much tougher to express in equivalent dollars. Just how much *is* the key to the executive washroom worth? How about the use of a corporate jet? The size of an office or the access to the company store is easier to measure, but you get the idea. Generally speaking even "Perks" can be matched by another company and are no guarantee against a raid by a headhunter.

>Long-Term Capital Accumulation or Deferred Compensation has the identifying characteristic of not being currently taxable, and that in turn means there are

strings attached to the benefit such that the beneficiary gets control only in the future and, if circumstances change, may not get the benefit at all. The prime example is the usual pension plan, but there are many others such as stock options, savings plans or just plain future payment for whatever reason so long as the payee has no control until the payment is made. Deferred compensation is harder for the raider to match. Strange as it may seem, the politicians have now decided that deferred compensation is somehow evil (I suppose because it isn't currently taxable and they can't get their hands on the money) and by legislation are gradually making it more and more difficult to make compensation deferred.

Psychic or "Ego" Compensation takes many forms, but usually has no determinable dollar value. It consists of items like a title, a portrait in the lobby, a seat on the Board of Directors without compensation or having one's name listed on the lobby directory. On a more practical level it may be being named "Salesman of the Month" or winning a Grammy Award or even being given "free time" to do some innovative research. You can think of many others. The key element is recognition for accomplishment without direct financial benefit.

Now let's consider how these various types of compensation may be used by the manager to get people to do what is wanted. Just what is it that can be achieved by compensation? For the individual one can think of the following:

> Basic living requirement.
> Luxury expenditures.
> Security including provision for disability.
> Estate accumulation.

Tangible measure of recognition of performance.
Psychological satisfaction or ego support.

For the corporation or other institution they boil down to only five:

Secure the number and the quality of people required to fill the various jobs in the organization.

Make personnel on the job as productive as possible. i.e. as a motivating force for individual effort including growth in job skills.

Protect against the loss of key people once the key people have been identified.

Direct effort toward institutional objectives.

Keep the individual from worrying about extraneous matters so he or she can concentrate on the job.

Each of these goals requires a somewhat different combination of compensations although quite obviously some elements have merit in every case.

SECURE THE NECESSARY PERSONNEL TO FILL THE POSITIONS

It should be apparent that getting quality personnel is *more* than a question of adequate compensation. Recruiting the proper people is as much a question of defining the position to be filled and identifying the characteristics of the person needed as it is a question of compensation. C. Northcote Parkinson in his admirable little book *Parkinson's Law* (John Murray, London 1957) points out and I quote, "Only a little thought is required to convince us that the perfect advertisement would attract only one reply and that from the right man." However, the total pay package has to be competitive or the candidate won't accept the position. This truism applies whether one is hiring a sweeper, a counter person at McDonald's, a museum curator or the president of a major corporation. Put in another way, a person who is qualified to be a sweeper won't make a good president of a company no matter how much the pay, and vice versa!

There have been volumes written on position descriptions (including a chapter in this book), job evaluations, salary and wage surveys, relative worth indices etc.,etc. and I don't propose to discuss these techniques here. The message I do want to leave is that the package of straight dollar compensation and "current" fringe benefits has to be at the going regional rate for the position in question or one will not get the quality of personnel required. Within limits one can insist on better-than-average candidates for any given position if the compensation package is better than average. Let me emphasize that simply paying better-than-average compensation will not result in above-average personnel. One gets the better people by defining the position in the first place, sticking to high standards in hiring and in performance, and in making the job psychically rewarding to the person.

When the effort is to lure someone away from an essentially equivalent position in another firm or organization, it will probably be necessary to pay a premium just to offset the risk a person runs in leaving a job where he or she is performing well to go to another location where there is no assurance of success. This premium in straight salary dollars and cents should be no more than what might be made up in one salary review cycle. If it takes more premium than that to get the person you want, the extra amount should be paid as a hiring bonus or in the arrangements for paying expenses due to moving rather than getting the premium built into the regular compensation framework where it affects all the other people in the organization. In many cases it is a matter of matching the package one is willing to offer to the specific needs of the person. The more unique the requirements of the position being filled, the more reason to tailor a compensation package to the candidate.

Certainly the security part of compensation has to be kept in mind and often the only "premium" required is a liberal, pre-defined, termination settlement in case the job doesn't work out in say the first year.

MAKING PERSONNEL PRODUCTIVE

The second use of compensation is to make personnel more productive, in other words incentive compensation or compensation which is variable with performance. In its simplest form it is called "piecework" and an employee is paid so much per piece produced. There are plenty of variations as to exactly what constitutes a "piece", but all forms of straight commission or direct payment based on measured units are piecework. In straight—forward jobs where units can be measured and related to the person producing them, this is a very effective form of compensation, but satisfactory results are dependent on maintaining the quality of the work product and in being able to tie "production" directly to the person being paid. The literature is full of how to set up and manage incentive schemes of this type, but there are a couple of principles that apply whether the incentive is applied to a factory production job or whether it is applied to the star life insurance salesman.

> Any straight incentive scheme must result in competitive compensation for normal or standard output. In other words there must be a fair day's pay for a fair day's work as a result of the working of the plan.

> There must be no question about how "production" (or "performance") is measured and everyone should be able to calculate his or her earnings based on information available to the person working under the scheme.

The productive person should be able to earn extra compensation in the range of 10-20% above the norm if the incentive scheme is to be effective. If the good person can't earn a bonus, the plan will not be an incentive.

There should be no cap on the amount that can be earned as the result of the working of a straight incentive scheme. If earnings are ridiculously out of range, it means that the system itself was not thought out or that the unit on which the bonus is paid is not being properly measured.

An incentive scheme which does not result in a competitive compensation package for acceptable productivity can only mean that good people will leave the job. A straight incentive scheme should not be a way of paying sub-standard wages. Likewise, unless the productive person can earn 10-20% above the base, the scheme will fail to be an incentive. There should be no cap on the amount that can be earned in this type of plan because a properly designed "piecework" scheme has its own cap based on what a person can accomplish whether that person is an hourly employee or the top-paid executive in the company. One test of such a plan is to ask oneself whether it is economically sound to have an unlimited pay-out as a result of the workings of the plan. In a properly conceived plan, the more an individual earns, the better! On the other hand, to have a cap on the plan sends a signal to the participants that once earnings go up, the plan will be changed and/or it is not really expected or desirable to get as much work product as possible.

People put caps on plans because they believe that the participants will find ways to "beat" the plan and annul the benefits to the company. There is no doubt that participants will try to do that and the way to face the problem is to make it quite clear from the beginning that the plan will be changed if conditions change. Incentives should only be paid for better than expected performance due to the *extra* effort or skill of the employee. So-called incentive compensation should not be paid for just doing one's job and if incentives can be earned without extra effort or skill because the conditions on the job have changed, no matter what the job is, then the plan should be changed and this should always be a well-understood condition of establishing the plan in the first place. Likewise, if astronomical bonuses can be earned without extraordinary effort, the plan was either faulty or the conditions have changed and in either case the plan should be changed. A corollary of this same idea is that incentive should be paid for attaining desired goals and it is a prerogative of the management to determine what those goals are. For example it may be more important for the company to increase the volume of product A this six months and product B the next six months. Obviously incentive should be paid for product A in the first six months and then changed to pay for product B in the second six months. In a non-industrial situation it may be desirable to reduce the backlog of applications this month and to speed up the payment cycle next month. Again, the incentive in month one should be focused on the number of applications in the backlog and next month on number of days average for payment. Incentive plans should always be subject to change periodically because of changed conditions or objectives, but *not* just because the participants are earning big bonuses! It is important to realize with plans of this type that the relationship an individual perceives between *effort* and rewards may influence his job motivation more than the relationship he perceives between *performance* and rewards. The participant has to understand and appreciate that it is *performance* from *extra* effort that gets rewarded.

DIRECT EFFORT TOWARD INSTITUTIONAL OBJECTIVES

Many incentive schemes are set up to reward group effort or for some nebulous goal like "improving company profits" or "increasing efficiency". Schemes like stock options are included in this category based on the idea that superior performance will result in improved value for the corporation's common stock and thus reward the participant. Generally speaking these schemes are useful incentives for only those few individuals whose decisions actually effect the way a company's stock value is perceived and even they are at the whim of general market trends. (At the moment options in dot.com companies have made many persons rich—at least on paper. History shows that the stock market is a fickle mistress and bubbles have a way of bursting!) For all the rest of the participants either the plan is no incentive at all or is a brief lift should they get a windfall from stock action beyond their control. (It may even have middle managers cheering for a takeover effort just because of the windfall on their options!). Said in another way when the pay-out of an incentive plan results from circumstances beyond the partici- pants control, it is not an incentive plan; it's a *lottery*! These plans have no place in the ordinary manager's scheme of things.

The most effective way to reward group effort and to get coopera- tion among the members of the group is to choose some specific objec- tive with a medium-term time frame and then define a formula that applies to selected and named participants in a way which all can understand. For example:

> For each new restaurant opened over the next eighteen months and which is generating an operating profit with- in 90 days after opening, an amount of $15,000 will be placed in a"kitty" to be paid on November 1, 200X split among the following participants per the percentages shown next to their names.

or:

> 8% of the increase in operating profit in the first six months of this year compared to the same period last year will be placed in a fund to be split equally among the fol- lowing named participants.

or:

> For every ton of Y product produced, sold and delivered between now and December 1st $10 will be put into a prize fund to be split 30% to Production Management

Dept. 410, 30% to Transportation Dept.411 and 40 % to Sales Dept. 412. The manager of each of the named departments will determine the split for the personnel of his department.

or:

For each vacation cruise package sold by March 15th an amount equal to 3% of the invoiced value will be placed in a kitty to be divided equally among the travel consultants in the Cedar Street office.

Similar bonus schemes can be thought up for even the smallest department or group of people. The characteristic of each of these schemes is a fixed reward for a specified result important to objectives of the organization paid to a defined group of individuals for activity within a fixed period of time. Incentives of this type need not be legalistic or complicated since there are no complicated tax rules which must be complied with. The scheme is self-terminating and may be renewed or modified depending on what the goals are at the time the plan has run its course.

In those cases where profit performance is to be used as the measure, it is important to relate incentive either to improvement over previous performance or some clear and understandable target and to the relative difficulty of reaching the goal. In multi-unit operations not evaluating this situation can easily result in *disincentive.* For example, top management often relates the size of a division's bonus pool to sheer amount of profit without considering the difficulty of getting the performance. Managers in a perennial money-loser may receive no incentive payment while those in a division with good profits may receive handsome bonuses. Yet, the management of the profitable division might be doing a relatively poor job of attaining the potential or could be losing ground to competition while the management of the unprofitable division could be effecting an heroic turnaround! Obviously this same comparison occurs between departments or even between smaller groups inside a department in any kind of an organization, commercial or institutional. Fair play and consistency are absolutely essential in any compensation scheme. Inconsistency destroys the fabric of a society faster than almost any vice. If one sector feels it isn't getting a fair deal, that's where the revolution starts!

A special case for incentive compensation has to do with salesmen or other similar employees who are paid a base salary and then are paid extra compensation based on some formula related to performance. (in the following example I am using a commercial salesman, but the same rules apply to a bank loan officer or a government adjustor or any similar activity) In my experience the most satisfactory way to deal with this case is to let the individual set his own goals for his territory or performance. For example, in preparation for a session with an individual to set sales goals for the next period, (this ought to be as often as every three months to be really effective) draw up a list of all the customers or clients and the sales to these customers in the same period for the two prior years. Sit down with the salesman and ask him to write down next to the customer's name what he thinks he will sell to each customer in the next period. This dollar figure almost without exception will be larger than you require for your own budget goal thus giving you the opportunity to say something like:

> "That's fine, Sam, and now just to make sure you will make your estimate, I'll start paying you bonus at 80% of the sales total you have just indicated. You will get extra compensation at 5% of sales over $XXX which is 80% of the total on the list here. Just so we understand each other, a sale is a sale when the invoice has been sent out. Any bad debts in your accounts will be charged against your sales total when the account is 90 days overdue and all returns will be charged against your sales when the customer takes the credit. "Sales" are gross sales as reported on the monthly sales report which is the one you always work

with. The bonus you earn will be paid 10 days after the books are closed for the quarter. Is that fair?"

Obviously, if Sam agrees, the deal should be confirmed to him in writing and in the same simple terms used in your discussion. In the example, I have assumed that 80% of the sales estimate is good enough for *your* plan and that anything more represents better than average performance and worth a bonus. (Quite obviously the same technique could be applied to a loan officer in a bank by making the bonus payable on loans "approved by the loan committee" with whatever other conditions are appropriate.) If Sam's estimate is not good enough or if the market has changed in a way that is beyond the control of the salesman, some other goal must be set. The important point is that bonus should be paid for better than normal performance as a result of above normal effort.

PROTECTING AGAINST LOSS OF KEY PEOPLE

A much tougher task for compensation is using it properly to protect against the loss of key people at any level. Non-financial compensation may be the most important element in that package and while titles and "perks" are important, they are not so important to the key people as job satisfaction, but more about that in a moment. The key to developing a compensation package to deter "pirating" of personnel is to have elements which are not easily matched by the "pirate" or are so expensive to match that the price is too high. Certainly straight salary can be matched with a simple phone call naming a higher figure. It is not so easy to match several years' payments into a company-matched savings plan where the penalty for early withdrawal is the loss of company payments. In other words those forms of compensation that result in estate building are the ones which, as time goes by, are more and more difficult for the pirate to match. Cancelling options is a usual practice although the pirating company can more easily match options. What they can't match is the gain which may already exist in the options.

And now a word about job satisfaction. It all starts with a good understanding between the employee and his boss about what performance is expected on the job, followed by seeing that the employee has the resources to do that job. In some positions, as for example a research physicist, that means a properly equipped laboratory, in other positions it may mean being given the authority required to get results without being second-guessed, or it may mean being relieved of some tasks in order to make time available for those things the employee really wants to do. In a university it may be lightening a teaching load in order to allow time for scholarship. More often than not the "recruiting pirate" is successful because the key employee is unhappy with his job conditions rather than because he is unhappy with his compensation package. (See the chapter on the How'm I Doing? talk.) In every case it means understanding what is involved in the job and seeing that public recognition is given for good performance. There can be job satisfaction in carrying out an assignment which is frustrating because proper resources are *not* available so long as that fact is recognized and proper credit is given for getting the job done "in spite of". For many people there is a lot of psychic satisfaction in doing the "impossible". Certainly job assignments have to be tailored to the individual. One doesn't choose a person who hates to travel and be away from home to be a traveling representative. Almost *no* amount of money will keep that person on the job for long. On the other hand asking someone who likes to travel and has been accustomed to seeing London, Paris and Rome as part of his job to settle down in Keokuk, Iowa in a regional office is certain trouble. Some people like the joys of administrative detail, others don't; some people like to work nights, others don't; some people like to make decisions, others don't; some people need to have their egos massaged frequently, others don't; some people are very sensitive to the trappings of office, others are not—these are some of the things which add up to job satisfaction. The good manager is aware of the differences and works them into management of the "compensation package".

Dr. Salk, the inventor of the first polio vaccine never made a vast fortune because he chose not to patent the vaccine and dedicated it to the general good. Still, his prestige brought him something more valuable than wealth in his eyes namely, the Salk Institute for Biological Studies in Torrey Pines, California. It is now considered one of the great intellectual treasures of the world and Dr. Salk got more satisfaction from working there under the stimulating conditions than any amount of money would have brought him.

THE NET-NET

While everyone likes to talk about compensation and the media particularly loves to make much of the compensation package of the highly paid, many salaried employees honestly can't tell one how much they are getting paid as a total package. They usually know what the take-home pay amounts to, they usually know whether they are covered by health insurance, but they ordinarily have little idea how much that is worth. They usually know whether there is a pension plan, but not what its monetary value is. Except for vacation allowances any other benefits are pretty sketchy. Very few employees can actually describe the details of fringe benefit plans and certainly have only a vague idea of the actual pay-off of the pension plan until they get right down to retiring. They may know about an institutional savings plan because they have seen an annual statement, but they usually are a little vague about exactly how it all works. Much more important in the day-to-day scheme of things is job satisfaction and that is a result of a complex of factors making up the entire environment. No compensation package by itself will make a happy and productive employee, but an unfair or inequitable package will quickly make an employee unhappy and non-productive!

It is up to the manager to use compensation to get the maximum benefit both for the organization and for the employee. The manager does that by understanding and thinking about the elements that make up a compensation package and then using them effectively.

Part II

WORKING WITH OTHERS IN THE ORGANIZATION

CHAPTER 10

WORKING WITH A SECRETARY

There is no doubt that a secretary can be about as important to your success as any other factor. Start out from the beginning thinking of your secretary as an "executive assistant" and that state of mind will get the relationship off on the right foot. This is no place for compromise—your secretary must simply be the *best* you can get.

There are many qualities you should be looking for in a secretary, but the first is **intelligence** and I mean quick, street-smart, active intelligence rather than some academic type ability. You want someone who has a quick mind: quick to understand what you want, quick to grasp a situation, quick to respond and with the associated memory which means he or she will remember what has been done, said, or filed.

The second quality is a pleasant, **out-going personality**. Your secretary is going to have to represent you to the world in some difficult situations. You should feel confident that your secretary is going to have, and will always present, an image you can be proud of whether in person or on the telephone. It is a common failure of secretaries, especially executive secretaries, to take on a "bossy" attitude or a "superior" attitude particularly with the more junior people or those whom the secretary judges to be out of favor. Don't allow it! Equal opportunity and equal treatment should start with your secretary and *you* should be sure that principle is understood and practiced.

It is also a common failing for a secretary to over-emphasize the importance of what the boss is doing or just how important in the general scheme of things the boss may be. It is a natural failing because it adds to the secretary's own status to believe the boss is important. Your secretary can protect your time and your schedule without being officious about it. We have all had the experience with the dentist or doctor whose receptionist thinks only her boss has a schedule to follow! How much better to hear a secretary saying, "I know he would want to see you, but looking at his calendar, he just doesn't have a moment free until tomorrow afternoon at 3:00. Would that be a convenient time for you?" rather than a blunt, "He can see you tomorrow at 3:00" with *no* smile and *no* explanation.

Telephone manners and tone are particularly important because this often is the first contact an outsider may have with you. It is one thing when an associate who knows and appreciates you is mishandled by your secretary; it is another when a person you don't even know is treated badly. There are plenty of good manuals on telephone procedures and manners. It is up to you to insist that your secretary practices what is being preached! If you are not sure, it is even worth having a friend make a call and report back with comment and suggestions.

The third quality might be called **professionalism**. Your secretary should take pride in doing things correctly and should just naturally be a perfectionist. He or she will be responsible for much that comes out of your office and the work product should always be top quality. All the simple things: proper format, no misspelled words, on time, etc. etc. should be routine. Certainly today a secretary need not be a prize-winner at shorthand, but he or she must be able to handle a word processor and simple computer tasks, maintain a schedule, deal with travel plans, understand standard procedures, maintain files, draft routine letters, keep your expense account, etc. etc. and do these tasks correctly. Included in being professional is the quality of being able to keep one's mouth shut. Your secretary should never talk with *anyone* about what is going on in your office or about what you have written or said. There is no way your secretary can be as useful as he or she should be if you have to keep any "secrets" because the person can't be trusted. You should feel that your associates have no reserve about leaving messages with your secretary, i.e. they should also feel there will be no "leaks" from that source. This is not to say that you must tell your secretary everything or that there aren't things which are better left unsaid or recorded only in a strictly personal file, but you **must be confident** that what your secretary knows goes no further. Don't underestimate the pressure that may be put on your secretary to reveal information: "Is there going to be a lay-off?" "Are we working the day after Thanksgiving?" "Is there going to be a Christmas party?" "When will the bonus checks be out?" or even more subtly, "Where in Europe did he say he was going?" before any trip has been announced. Again, there are plenty of good manuals on being an executive secretary and that isn't the purpose of this chapter. This chapter is to establish in you a state of mind about what you should expect in your secretary. The point to emphasize is that *your* secretary must be professional and of real assistance to you rather than a problem.

The last essential quality is that of being **responsible**. Some people just seem to have this attribute naturally as part of their character and that is what you want. It has been my experience that you find this quality in the daughter who is taking care of her aging mother or the man who is raising his brother's orphaned children, and you should look for these signs in the hiring interview. It is a personal trait and invaluable in a secretary. I don't have to dwell on this point because the reader certainly has his own examples of individuals who are responsible, but I want to emphasize that it is this trait that makes your secretary take *personally* his or her involvement in your affairs and it is this trait that makes a person put in the extra effort to accomplish some assignment when difficulties show up.

Now that you have chosen a secretary how do you work with that person? Start out with the little things, How does your secretary like to be addressed? Most companies have established traditions and you would do well to be as formal as is acceptable. It is quite standard to address a secretary by that person's first name when speaking to them, but to refer to them in the presence of others more formally, e.g. "Mary, would you please show Mr. Jones to the elevator." but, "Miss Smith will show you to the elevator, Mr. Jones." Even though it is customary to address the secretary by the first name, it is also customary that you be addressed more formally as Mr., Mrs. or Miss. Just the little touch of respect and discipline makes for a better working relationship over the long haul. Respect is what your secretary is looking for and what you should want as well.

A second small point is the way you like to have your mail organized. Tell your secretary how you want it done. Don't expect him or her to guess and *don't* put up with something that annoys you in any of the office routine. (There is much more on "Getting Organized" in a later chapter) As the old saying goes, "Your secretary is working for you. You are not working for your secretary!" Completely aside from that fact, minor annoyances if allowed to continue take nervous energy and will decrease your effectiveness.

Likewise, you should go over the other office routines which you want to specify like who (the boss, your spouse) shall have the privilege of interrupting when you are in a meeting or have others with you. How you wish to have the telephone answered and what you wish to do about telephone interruptions. All of these details don't have to be taken care of at once, but it is important that you have free and open discussions with your secretary about all aspects of the office routine and that he or she understand this is a two-way street. Your secretary may have some very good ideas about how to improve effectiveness, but you will have to ask!

It is a good plan to have a regular time each day to go over the day's work with your secretary. Either first thing in the morning or just after the morning mail is delivered are good times. You may also want to schedule a regular session in mid or late afternoon. For this session you should be prepared with a list of things you want to have done or want to discuss and your secretary should be prepared with matters for which he or she wants instructions or decisions. Of course your secretary will have your calendar at hand and will remind you of appointments, dead-lines or anything else about which you should be aware. (Your secretary should feel responsible for seeing that you answer that memo or prepare that report when a deadline or commitment is involved and should give you a timely reminder.) Both of you will work more effectively with a regularly scheduled time than with sporadic interruptions as questions arise. It's a good trick to simply jot a note about something you want to discuss but can postpone until your regular session. Actually handwritten notes to your secretary can often save time for both of you; use them often.

Try to give your secretary as much responsibility as that person can handle and you will be freed for more important things. You should be able to say, "Get me to Chicago on Tuesday in time for a 10:30 A.M. meeting." and know that your secretary will get you on the airline you favor, will arrange for getting you to the airport, will, if necessary, check the Chicago address and telephone for instructions on how to get there from the airport, will arrange for a hotel or a return flight as appropriate, will check to see that you have funds, will prepare your docket and see that you have airline tickets and everything else you may need.

You should be able to hand over a piece of correspondence saying, "Tell them, no." and know that a well-written letter in your usual style will appear ready for your signature. Certainly your secretary can plot graphs, keep production records, or otherwise handle special projects of that type including the routine on the computer. I might add that a secretary doesn't have to be chained to the desk. If there is something to be researched in the library, the need to get opinions from a number of different people, or the task of obtaining figures from the factory, your secretary may well be able to do the job. He or she should know how to access locally available data via the computer and know how to get at any web sites you use regularly. The more a secretary can take on, the more interesting the job and the more help to you. In other words try to make your "secretary" an "assistant" rather than just a word processor or the keeper of your appointment calendar. It almost goes without saying that he or she should be even more computer literate than you are! Much of what you want from the computer or the internet, your secretary should be able to get for you.

Here are a few practical points:

> As soon as convenient, have your spouse get to know your secretary.

> When appropriate, introduce your secretary to visitors. It is a recognition of your secretary's importance to you and a sign of respect. It also gives the visitor a contact point in case you are not available at some future time.

Let your secretary manage the general files and hold him or her responsible for knowing where to find documents. This includes being able to access information from the computer and LAN.

The office should always be immaculate and in order when work is complete or when the day is done. No files left around, no coffee cups, no mess and nothing on top of the file cabinets. Again, part of the way people judge you is the way your office looks and your secretary's surroundings are part of that picture.

Exchange keys so you can get into the files and into your secretary's desk if necessary, and so your secretary can get into your desk and files. Respect the privacy of your secretary's desk and don't go rooting around in it unless absolutely necessary.

Set the dress code promptly. Your secretary should dress on the conservative side whether male or female.

Your secretary's desk should not be the center for the morning "coffee-klatsch". The atmosphere should always be all-business. Likewise personal phone conversations should be brief. If a lengthy conversation is unavoidable, your secretary should go to some other phone. No personal business on the computer terminal without specific permission.

If two phone lines are available, it is usually better to have your secretary's line be the one that is public and known to outsiders reserving your own line for inside use only. He or she will then monitor all outside calls.

A good secretary is a prize. Keep the job interesting by continuing to challenge the person in it. You will be surprised by how much that person can do to make your job easier. You may even be surprised to find out just how much of your job a good secretary can actually do leaving you time for new initiatives.

CHAPTER 11

MANAGING A BOSS

Not everyone understands the cardinal principles of managing a boss and there are only three:

> Conduct yourself in such a way that your boss "Looks Good".

> It is up to *you* to get along with your boss, not the other way around.

> Bosses are human, too.

Almost everything in your relationship with your boss can be related to these three maxims. Most people don't like to think about the fact that most of us spend our lives as "subordinates". It is a very privileged few (if one excludes the self-employed) who have no "superior"to whom they report.

LOOKING GOOD

The first rule in making your boss look good is, "No Surprises!" You must keep your boss informed on those things he or she should know, both good *and* bad. particularly in case of bad news, you must let him or her know promptly. If you tell your boss as soon as there is trouble, all he or she can say is, "What can I do to help?". On the other hand, if the news comes from some other channel, not only may it embarrass your boss, but he or she has every right to be upset with your performance.

The second part of making your boss look good is to be sure *you* understand what he or she wants you to do. There are really two kinds of tasks to be carried out. The first is the regular routine tasks which should be clear from your position description. The position description was discussed in detail in the chapter on that subject, but you should have one on which you and your boss have agreed. If you faithfully carry out the responsibilities listed in the description, you will be doing what your boss wants as far as the usual job goes.

The other kind of task is one that is assigned for whatever reason. Never hesitate to question or to re-state an order or assignment so you are certain of what is wanted. You make your boss look *bad* when you have to say, "But I *thought* this was what you wanted." In taking on an assignment if there is a conflict with some other duty or event, be certain your boss understands. Either say or clarify by memo the consequences of the conflict. For example:

> "In order to prepare the 1986 budget figures by next Tuesday as you requested, I'll have to postpone until next Wednesday the meeting in Detroit with Jones. Unless I hear otherwise from you by noon tomorrow when I should let Jones know, I'll assume you want me to prepare the budget."

A variation on this same theme comes when you know you will not get an assignment done by a promised date. If you tell your boss you will have something done by a certain time and it will not be done, tell him or her *as soon as you know* and set a new date and time when the task will be done. You never know what your boss has promised *his* or *her* boss!

Another type of "surprise" comes when you have to deviate from approved policy or exceed your limits of authority in order to take care of some unusual situation. While you can't actually avoid the surprise, you must immediately let your boss know the circumstances and the decision or action which you had to take. Again, it's possible that what was done exceeded his or her authority as well.

An important part of making your boss look good is to make certain that your work, especially anything your boss is going to make use of, is always up to standard. No sloppy work! You must always take a second look at any work product going to your boss especially when one of your subordinates has been involved in the preparation. Secretaries make typos, lab assistants may leave out a crucial set of figures, and so it goes. Is there a page missing? Do the figures make sense? Do the graphs have labels? Read the report one last time before you send the work off. As far as your boss is concerned, if your signature is on it, it is *your* work. To the extent that your work product is just plain sloppy or does not meet your boss' standards, you have added to his or her workload and that is *bad*.

People rise in organizations for different reasons. You must know and appreciate the area of your boss' expertise. Having this understanding gives you the chance to make available your own background in any area in which you are more knowledgeable than your boss. This help makes him look good and may make for closer collaboration.

IT'S UP TO YOU TO GET ALONG

Back to the second cardinal principle, "It is up to you to get along with your boss, not the other way around." There is no requirement that a boss be superhuman. He or she can be handsome or ugly, fat or thin, of any faith, of any ethnic background. *Your* boss is what he or she is, warts and all, and deserves respect for the position he or she holds. Getting along with the boss starts with an appreciation of the qualities which got that person into the job in the first place. If you don't have a high opinion of your boss, it may well be that you don't understand his or her good points or you don't understand what the job really involves.

Once you have been on your job for a while, you should know your boss' habits and schedule. What is even more important, you should be able to anticipate his or her needs. By taking the initiative to provide your boss with a report or the draft of a plan which you believe could be useful, you help your chances of learning from him or her. In initiating such work, think about it from the viewpoint of the boss. The more closely your style conforms to that of your boss and the more exactly the work suits his or her way of thinking, the more useful it is both to your boss and as a training for you. Try to learn something every time you meet with the boss.

Be ready if the boss is in the habit of coming into your department every morning to see how things are going. Not only should you have on hand whatever facts and figures the boss likes to see on a regular basis, but this is the time to bring up problems on which you want advice or decisions. You should at that time call his or her attention to anything that is out of the ordinary or anything that might come as a surprise. While you will undoubtedly mention the good things like a new production record or an outstanding exhibit, your boss is really looking for problems and the bad news. The good news can wait.

It is likely that your boss will meet with you in a more formal way on a regular schedule to discuss whatever is on his or her mind. You should be sensitive to the protocol and arrange your "To Discuss" folder in the order your boss likes to handle items. The folder should contain a prioritized list of subjects you wish to bring up. It should also contain copies of the memos you suspect may trigger further conversation. Having all this in place gives you a chance to be ready for a meeting even if called at other than the regular scheduled time. You have no right to waste your boss' time by being unprepared for any working session. Learn the manner in which he or she likes material presented. If the boss likes pictures, use pictures. If he or she likes graphs, use graphs.

BOSSES ARE HUMAN, TOO

If you have a great boss and a fine relationship, you are fortunate. About the only question you should be asking yourself is, "Am I learning as much as I can from this person, or am I just enjoying the easy relationship?" On the other hand, suppose your relationship is poor for whatever reason: Your boss refuses to give out any information beyond the bare essentials needed for your job. He or she reaches past you to give instructions to your people as though you were unable to do it or weren't in the picture. He or she is just downright unfriendly. You must first try to decide where the problem lies. Machiavelli may give some guidance here. He says in *The Prince*, "Men do you harm either because they fear you or because they hate you."

If the problem comes from your being looked on as a threat, you can improve the relationship, no matter how prickly the boss may be, by showing that you respect him or her and want to learn as much as possible from the person. It is most important not to return the ill feeling. By that I mean that openly showing you have a low opinion of the boss or discussing presumed shortcomings with others only confirms the suspicion that you are a threat. Avoid reciprocating the boss' attitude. Search out and talk about what interests him or her. Look for some quality in the person you can genuinely appreciate. Avoid arguments or other confrontations, but if one must occur, be certain it is in the privacy of an office. Be business-like and friendly in all your inter-personal dealings. Your actual behavior is the clue to your intentions.

If it is not clear what the problem in your relationship with the boss is, or if you don't know what to do about it, then you have to have a "How'm I Doing" session. This time you are the subject. Remember, this kind of discussion can't be held when you are angry. It is not a question of who's right and who's wrong. What you are trying to do is clear up a relationship between two people who have to work together and *that* can only be done by focusing on the elements and not on personalities. You must be as specific as you can about what is bothering you. You must *listen* to what your boss says in the "How'm

I Doing" session and then work at it until there is an understanding. It may be that your boss is unwilling to change or unwilling to understand what is bothering you. In that case if you can't tolerate the problem, you may have to resign or ask for a transfer to another department. Never, repeat *never*, tender your resignation unless you are ready to have it accepted! You may not be as indispensable as you think and this action may even start the boss thinking about your replacement for the first time! Especially if there is a big difference in years of service, higher management is more likely to stand behind your boss than to take your position no matter how right you think you are.

The whole problem may just be a question of style. You will see in the chapter on "A Little Career Planning" we talk about company culture. Perhaps your boss represents a culture with which you are uneasy. You may consider him or her "disorganized" because he or she prefers to "drop-in" rather than scheduling formal meeting times, or perhaps pays no attention to chain of command or telephones night or day whenever the mood strikes and just generally seems unpredictable. If you are the type that doesn't like the unexpected, a loosely run organization is not for you. On the other hand, perhaps you are the one who frets at structure. The boss seems too rigid, unwilling to take chances or try anything new. He or she always follows "the book" no matter what the consequences. There is no freedom of action, no chance for initiative. Whichever the case, your style and the boss' style are at odds. It is unlikely that you will be able to change the way your boss does business especially if he or she is conforming to the basic culture of the institution. You may be able to modify one or two aspects by talking the problem over, but by and large, you either have to adapt or get out! It is just possible that in this particular institution and under these particular conditions, the boss is right and you are wrong. Before you condemn the whole scene, step back, reconsider and see whether you haven't learned something of value.

Again, Machiavelli has some advice for us. "When trouble is sensed well in advance, it can be easily remedied; if you wait for it to show itself, any medicine will be too late because the disease will have become incurable." If you and your boss are not getting along, resolve the problem as soon as it is detected.

One of the more difficult situations is a result of the operation of the maxim stated by Dr. Laurence J. Peter and Mr. Raymond Hull authors of C.Northcote Parkinson's *Peter Principle,* "In a hierarchy every employee tends to rise to his level of incompetence" and the corollary, "In time, every post tends to be occupied by an employee who is incompetent to carry out his duties". If this describes your boss, you still must do all that you can to make him or her look good short of out-right cover-up. It is more than likely that top management is well aware of the problem; *you* may even be their hope for an answer. It is up to you to identify those areas where your boss is incompetent and proceed with that knowledge always in mind. It may be that his or her technical skills have become obsolete, but judgement may still be excellent. Make use of the judgement and avoid the technical skills. Perhaps the person is fine so long as everything is routine and going along smoothly, but goes to pieces under stress. In that case you must be prepared to go it alone or seek other support when things go wrong. Whatever the weakness, it is up to you to find ways to cope. It is *not* your place to "spread the word" or start agitating to get the person removed.

Writing about bosses has been a favorite subject for psychologists. They have categorized them as "Bullies", "Workaholics", "Perfectionists", "Demanding", "Authoritarian", "Aloof" or just plain "Difficult". This may be due to the fact that the psychologists have never had a *good* boss. What is certain is that all bosses are human! Most of them are pretty fine folk who are dedicated to their jobs and concerned about the people who work for them. Like all humans, they have problems and they have personalities. This is a two-way street. How you and your boss get along may be the toughest test of your own managerial ability!

CHAPTER 12

LIVING WITH ACCOUNTING AND ACCOUNTS

Now that you have your unit you will have to live with accountants, familiarly known as "bean-counters"! What follows is written with the commercial situation in mind, but all institutions, profit or non-profit, have books of account and the same thoughts apply wherever accounts are kept.

The "official" figures of a business are generated by accountants. They have the great misfortune, or so it seems to the rest of us mortals, of having to work under the *Generally Accepted Accounting Principles* plus regulations galore from the many government agencies together with a small dash of institutional precedent thrown in, "That's the way it has always been done around here and we *do* have to maintain comparability." On the other hand the accountants revel in the fact that they alone understand the mysterious conditions under which they work. It makes them members of a sort of secret club with passwords and rules which only they understand. The purpose of this chapter is to lift the veil on the mystery and to outline a few useful ways of working with the accounting staff.

Accountants are *supposed* to develop information for managers in the form of numbers which can be used to run the business or to manage the affairs of a non-profit organization. They also have to satisfy requirements for various reports to the public and to stockholders. Fortunately or unfortunately the financial types have to use *words* as well as numbers to get their various tasks done and that is where most of the problems come from. At the risk of insulting your intelligence, and theirs, let me just point out that fundamentally the way account-ants do their job is by establishing "accounts" to which they either credit or debit various transactions. At the end of some accounting period they summarize and analyze the balances in the accounts in order to come up with financial reports which then emerge from the financial services as the work product to be used by the rest of the organization. The problem comes both in the definition of the accounts and in deciding just what is to be credited or debited. While charts of accounts may look and sound very much alike, it is the words, the detailed definition of what is in an account, that cause the problems. Just what *is* the difference between "Gross Sales" and "Net Sales"? Just what *is* included in the "Direct Labor" account as contrasted to the "Indirect Labor" account? I think you can see what can happen and how important it is not to assume you know what is in an account just because it is labeled in English you think you understand. A cou-ple of examples of how a named account can be confusing will demon-strate why you must not "assume" what the actual account includes.

> UTILITIES—does this account include *all* gas electric and telephone or do some of these costs get recorded in an overhead account because they are "fixed". for example the electricity required just to light the parking lot, the building entrance and the halls may well be considered "fixed". While the electricity required for other operations would be charged this account. Is telephone included or is this expense recorded as "Communication Expense"?

> SUPPLIES—In the typical office this account may include paper clips, envelopes, scotch tape *but* probably does not

include computer discs, cartridges for printers or other similar expenses associated with data processing/computers.

When you ask the professional what is included in an account, he or she will answer by reading the words used in the formal Chart of Accounts. Unfortunately, to the ordinary person the definition is full of accounting jargon that either doesn't seem to make much sense or, if it does, probably has been misinterpreted! The only sure way to know is to sit down with your friendly accountant and get him to tell you in plain language and with examples of his postings just what the words mean. If it still doesn't make sense or if it doesn't reflect the way the unit operates, then it is time for some re-definition. No account is ever better than its definition.

Another problem has to do with how good the numbers are. All accounting numbers may look alike, but they have widely varying degrees of significance or validity and the good manager doesn't sit there fat, dumb and happy taking every number presented by the accountants as being equally valid or even correct. A good rule to work by is:

> "All Numbers one gets from accounts are wrong" It's only a question of how wrong they are and are they good enough for the task at hand.

Unfortunately numbers presented in accounting reports, or "statements" as the accountants like to call them, are all presented to at least two decimal points (in cents accounting) as though they were all of the same quality. We know that isn't the case and the significance of the figures depends both on the validity of the source information and on the accuracy of the data itself. If, for example, a labor cost is being developed from a time card made out by a certain individual, the labor rate is probably exactly right, but the amount of time spent on each task during the day depends on how good a job that person did in recording the information and whether or not he or she in fact got the various allowed classifications correct. Another example could be an accountant starting with data accurate to three places and then using some factor which results in a computation to six places. The last three digits of the resulting calculation have no significance. A usual case comes in the extension of estimates made for budgets or similar purposes. One develops an estimate of units to be sold which the accountant then multiplies by a sales price accurate to the last cent based on *present* selling prices. Obviously the resulting dollar figure is only as good as the estimate of units to be sold—say plus or minus 10% if the sales unit estimate is in fact that good. The validity is further compromised by the price used which can easily be off 10% either way depending on the market at the future time. If both are off in the same direction, the resulting figure is only as good as the product of the two estimates. If they were both off 10% in the same direction, the resulting forecast is only valid to 0.9 x 0.9 or 0.81 i.e. 81% of the figure shown. No need to beat this thought into the ground. The good manager uses accounting figures with caution and *thinks* about their validity. Just how good is the basic information on which the accounting reports are based?

This brings me to an important message: an accountant can be the manager's best friend. Get to know yours well. Long before the official monthly reports/statements are issued, your friendly accountant can let you know when he senses some problem. Often the problem results from the validity of the information he is working with e.g. he has been sent some incorrect figures from your section! It's a whole lot better for him and a whole lot better for you to get the figures right before he finalizes the reports for the month than to have them wrong for *two months*: this month because the input was wrong and next month because of the correcting entry. Accountants are not supposed to be creative; they work with the information they are given. It's up to you to see that the information is correct. On the other hand accountants are supposed to do more than just keep records. They should think about the figures as they process them and look for things that are inconsistent or don't make sense. What I'm saying is there is a two way street here. The manager must keep the accountant informed of changes in the operations which affect the way figures are reported or used and the accountant must keep the manager informed of patterns showing in the figures which can help the manager do a better job. When you get the report and it doesn't make sense to you, then you have a responsibility to let the accountant know. Perhaps some item got charged to the wrong place or someone missed a decimal point somewhere. Always "take a squint" at the report to see if it reflects what you know to be the case.

Just a word of caution—while much of what accountants do is utilized in financial control, it is not the same technique and takes a different mind-set. Accountants keep the books of account according to defined rules and with information supplied to them. Deal with them under their ground rules and you should find the relationship rewarding. Using the figures to control activities is *your* responsibility not that of your accountant.

Here are a few principles to observe:

> Make friends with your accountant. He or she can make life a lot simpler for you.

> Be *certain* you know the definition of the accounts with which you will be working and be sure you know exactly what is included in each account in actual practice.

> Don't trust any of the figures to be absolutely accurate. Learn to judge and to make use of the *quality* of figures.

> Do your part to make certain the input to the accounts is as accurate as possible under the circumstances.

> Always make the mental comparison between accounting and financial reports and what you *know* to be the actual

case. "Take a squint" at the net-net of any report or statement. Does it agree with the "real world" as you know it.

If you would like to know a great deal more about this whole subject, I recommend *The Controller's Handbook* edited by Sam Goodman
and James Reece and published in 1978 by Dow Jones—Irwin (ISBN
0-87094-157-7). It is what I call a "plain language" manual on all
aspects of the accounting/controller function as it applies to the
management task.

CHAPTER 13

WORKING WITH A LAWYER

In this increasingly regulated, legislated and litigious society, every-one has to be aware of and appreciate the complexities of law. The whole matter is further complicated by the growing international nature of business which brings into play the law and regulations of other sovereign countries. This is no game for an amateur! Lawyers will be a part of your life whether you like it or not. What follows is written from the commercial point of view, but the thoughts apply to any institution whether for profit or not. Any institution is governed by the appropriate law and all must be ready to work with lawyers.

Lawyers are specialists; they are a breed of their own and one has to learn to deal with them. Lawyers for their part have two big com-plaints about their relationship with non-legal "types". The first is that as lawyers they are brought into a situation too late, after problems have developed that could have been avoided had they been con-sulted from the beginning. The second complaint is that they are rarely given all the facts.

Let me illustrate the second point. Early in my career I went with a problem to a wise old lawyer, carefully presented my case and when I had finished, asked for his opinion. His reply was, "Based on what you have told me my opinion is..." followed by an opinion which was obviously way off the mark! I protested, "But so and so, and so and so are true so your opinion can't possibly be correct." To which his calm reply was, "Based on the additional facts you have given me, my opinion now is...". Still wide of the mark. So I blurted out the entire background of the matter and then got a sound opinion plus good advice on how to handle the situation in question.

My teacher, the wise old lawyer, was familiar with the kind of situation I had described to him and could easily have filled in the missing information himself, but he was doing me a great favor in teaching me that giving your lawyer part of the picture or only selected facts will result in poor legal advice. Most lawyers will not take the time to educate you and simply give an opinion based on what you have told them plus their own guess at the other facts of the situation which may or may not be correct. Certainly you owe it to yourself, and to your lawyer, to prepare carefully for any consultation and to be sure you have all the pertinent information. The best thing to do is to write up before any meeting a summary of the problem, the facts as you know them and the question on which you want an opinion.

On the other hand it is important to keep in mind that the lawyer is working for you not the other way around. You are his client and he owes you the benefit of his service. For example, suppose you are going to take part in a meeting or conference where your lawyer should be present. Make it clear at the outset how the meeting is to be handled. If you wish to do the talking, or are required by the circumstances to do the talking, your lawyer should address all of his comments or opinions to you: written notes. whispered advice. and not to the meeting at large. If required, it is better to ask for a recess to talk out some sticky point than to get the lawyer directly involved in the negotiations. This is not to say that there are not times when the lawyer should do all the talking, as for instance in a court trial proceeding. What I am saying is that you should be the one to decide who does the talking in any meeting outside a courtroom.

Lawyers are not an unmixed blessing when it comes to negotiations or dealing with other people. They have been trained to see the complications in any set of circumstances and this can well upset reaching of agreement by bringing extraneous details into the picture too soon. Lawyers also have some of the qualities of accountants in that they have been trained to be sticklers for form and detail. This can be upsetting to the businessman who wants to "get on with it", but the lawyers know should the matter ever get to a court, the form and the detail may, in fact surely will, become very important. The very focus on form and detail however brings with it the quality of inflexibility and lack of imagination which can interfere with the negotiating process. Particularly outside of the United States it is often a good idea to go into an initial negotiating meeting without your lawyer, but with a draft of the heads of an agreement (the basic points around which a deal can be constructed) from which an agreement in principle, subject to final draft by the lawyers, can be reached. If the basic structure of the deal can be set, then the lawyers can flesh out the details without upsetting the prime participants. If some particularly sticky point shows up as the details are worked out, the principals can go back to the agreement in principle in its simple form to work out whatever compromise is required. In the United States it is the practice to have long and detailed agreements full of "boiler plate". In the rest of the world this is not the case and the typical agreement drafted in the U.S. is looked on with great suspicion as being entirely too complicated for use between honorable businessmen! It is usually best to have a local firm do the final agreement when outside the United States. At the very least, if a U.S. firm is used, the lawyer should specialize in foreign work.

I don't want to suggest that the formal document is not needed just because one is dealing between honorable businessmen. It is often said, "No one needs a legal document so long as the relationship is running smoothly". The carefully drafted, legal document is important only when there is trouble, but when you need it, it is invaluable. However, there are many instances in the United States as well as abroad (where the Commercial Code controls the aspects of many transactions regardless of what is written in an agreement) where a formidable, legal document does more harm than good. In these cases a carefully drafted letter setting forth the deal with provision for a copy of the letter to be signed, dated and returned as indication of acceptance is more appropriate. Certainly in situations like ordinary employment or incentive plan commitments, a letter agreement sets a far better tone than a formal legal document full of "Whereas's". In the overseas situation it is very often the case that the entire deal rests on personal relationships and only the letter agreement is suitable.

Whatever the form, an agreement is an agreement and if you are the one signing or if you are recommending that your boss sign, don't take your lawyer's word for it, but *read the document yourself*. Legal documents have a way of getting "messed up" in the typing or in the drafting particularly in this day and age of computer-generated documents. If something goes wrong like a clause being added that doesn't belong in the document or worse yet an outright error in what is being agreed, you may be upset with the quality of your lawyer's work, but *he* isn't going to sign it, *you* are! Any errors are your ultimate responsibility.

Lawyers are technical specialists and not business men. While you should listen very carefully to their technical advice, the business decision has to be yours. It is the businessman's choice when it comes to risk. The lawyer can describe the possible extent of the risk or the penalties involved, but it is not his responsibility to take risk. Much of the time you will find in business situations that lawyer's opinions are not sharp and clear, but instead rather ambiguous full of "if's" and "maybe's". In many instances the case law or the regulations are not too clear or the particular course of action you are proposing may have had little precedent. Don't expect your lawyer's advice to be absolute, but you can certainly insist that his advice focus on *your* problem and not on one he dreams up. In any case one can, in the United States, be taken to court for almost anything whether in your opinion or your lawyer's opinion the case has merit or not. While you can't let your business judgement be unduly influenced by the chance of legal action, lawsuits are expensive and time-consuming. In a jury trial especially, one cannot predict what kind of a verdict will be rendered (that is why so many disputes are settled out-of-court). So the prudent course, even though *you* must make the decision, is to take your lawyer's advice seriously. However, it is *not* acceptable for your lawyer simply to say that what you propose to do can't be done. Rather it is his obligation to make clear to you how to structure a transaction so it can be done legally or to identify those elements of your proposal which are forbidden by law so you can modify them. Again, it is not the lawyer's prerogative to substitute his business judgement for yours.

Just as it is important for you to be sure your lawyer knows all the important facts in any case and that you have told him everything you know, it is essential that he do a proper job of preparing you to testify in case of an appearance before any court. The rules in a court are very specific and preparation should include exposing you to questions that may be asked and the proper way to reply to them. This is not to say that you should not be telling the truth when you are under oath, but knowing how to answer questions pertaining to the particular case at hand is extremely important and you should be cooperative.

Lawyers today are specialized just as physicians are specialized. Many firms are also specialized into what are known as "boutique firms" bankruptcy, personal injury, labor disputes, patents etc. Be sure that the lawyer you use is competent in the field for which his advice is being asked. You wouldn't go to a dermatologist for advice about your heart; don't go to an acquisition specialist for advice on patents and don't go to a patent lawyer for advice on labor law! In really large firms one usually finds both the general and specialized with the general lawyers maintaining the long-term relationship and calling in the various specialists as required by the circumstances. (If you are using an "outside" lawyer, it is a very sound practice to have a letter of agreement stating the terms under which the firm or the lawyer is being employed and perhaps specifying a cap on the ultimate fee. Such an agreement should also specify that once the particular case is complete, all material will be confidential and as many documents as possible returned. Such protection is especially important should the lawyer or the law firm later represent a competitor.) My lawyer friends tell me that the biggest problems between lawyers and their clients come over misunderstandings about billings. To keep these problems to a minimum it is important in retaining the services of a lawyer to specify three things:

> Who is the client, i.e from whom should he be taking orders or who makes the ultimate decisions.

> How much time should be spent on the case, i.e. just how important is this matter.

> When must the work be completed.

These factors are self-explanatory, but should be explicitly determined. The first, "Who is the client", is more likely to cause confusion in larger organizations where it is not always clear who must ultimately be satisfied that the matter at hand has been handled properly. The lawyer may not do his or her best work unless the ultimate client has taken part in the briefing. As for the second factor, the difference between an off-the-cuff opinion and a completely researched one can mean thousands of dollars in fees. It's *your responsibility* to decide which you want.

One final word. There is a test which anyone can apply to his actions that requires no lawyer and may save many headaches. If you *know* the intent of what you are proposing to do is dishonest, immoral, or illegal, regardless of how it may be dressed up, then don't do it! If the intent is to fix prices, no matter how elegant the scheme, it is illegal. If the intent is to defraud, no matter how sophisticated the proposal, it is illegal. Most people don't need a lawyer to tell them what their conscience can tell them and no one should expect a lawyer to tolerate or be a party to any criminal act.

As a professional manager perhaps the best way to think of a lawyer is in the role of a pilot helping you to navigate the complexities of legislative action, regulation and precedent in a manner that lets you accomplish your proposed course of action without going on the rocks!

Just a word about where the lawyer fits in when you are called before a court of law for whatever reason. Here the tables are reversed and the lawyer is on his "home court". Do what the lawyer tells you to do and don't try in court to substitute your judgement for that of your lawyer. Court procedures are complex and based on years of precedent. It's no place for the amateur. If you are to give a deposition, get fully instructed as to what is expected and *know your facts i.e., do your homework.* There are severe penalties for giving false testimony and you don't want to find out what they are! If there is any difference between what you believe to be the facts and what your lawyer is asking you to testify to, work it out before you are under oath. Above all, don't let the lawyer from the opposing side put words in your mouth. Don't argue; just insist that what is being proposed is not your position. Again, court proceedings follow very specific rules and procedures. Get a good lawyer and do as you are told!

CHAPTER 14

LIVING WITH A UNION

Sooner or later as a manager you will have to deal with "Labor Trouble". It is one thing when you are dealing directly with the person or people involved. Ordinarily just plain common sense and a fair, square deal will resolve the problem. It is quite another when you are dealing with "organized labor", i.e. a situation where you have to deal with your employees through the union and under the constraints of the labor laws. This chapter is about working with labor unions who represent your people although many of the thoughts are equally useful when your people are not represented by a union. These thoughts are equally applicable to profit and non-profit organizations.

In thinking about how to work with union representatives it is important to start with the fact that a union is a **political organization** and works from a different set of assumptions from those of the *business* or *functional* organization with which it is dealing. Union leaders behave like politicians and must be handled that way. Except in a few, usually corrupt, unions, the leaders derive their power from the people. They ordinarily think about a problem from the point of view of the entire body and how a solution will be viewed when the next election comes rather than the individual's particular circumstances. When they fail to do so, the people they represent repudiate them. That is why, for example, bargaining committees who think they have

made as good a deal as it is possible to make, can't always deliver rat-
ification from the rank and file. Don't trust a "sweetheart deal".
Eventually the rank and file will renege on it.

Before going on to the more specific situations it is well to emphasize that dealing with the union brings with it all the formalities of the
labor laws and even more specifically the restraints of the "Union
Contract" which is the formal document of the results of negotiations
between the employing organization and the union. Both for-profit
and non-profit organizations have union contracts. If your organization has one, one of your responsibilities as a new manager is to
become *thoroughly* familiar with it and with the associated procedures and policies. Don't just listen to what people tell you, but read
the actual documents. When there is a dispute, the written word carries a great deal of weight! You can be sure that the union representative will know what the words say.

There are two general situations in cases of labor trouble involving
the union. In one case the difficulty can be resolved through the grievance procedures perhaps even going so far as binding arbitration.
These cases usually involve individual instances. In the second situation the problem will be more general and may involve the union as a
whole—perhaps the negotiation of the initial contract after certifica-
tion of the union or failure to reach agreement on the renewal of an
expiring contract. In these latter cases after all efforts at mediation
have failed, a strike results!

I won't spend much time on situations which can be handled
through the grievance procedures, but let me say at the outset in
recognition of the political nature of the union rep's position, it is well
to let him or her win a few! Also, it is *very* important to take all grievances seriously and to avoid letting a backlog of unresolved cases
build up. To the person on the job an unresolved grievance can
become an all-consuming passion to the point where that person can't
think or talk about anything else. One of the advantages of having
union representation is the very fact that the union rep is likely to force
the manager to handle grievances promptly.

Let's first talk about the one grievance you don't want and can't afford to lose and that is a grievance over discharge or termination of employment. This doesn't mean you shouldn't fire people who deserve it, but it does mean that the process has to be done in the right way. (Terminating someone's employment is such a serious matter that the job should be done correctly whether there is a grievance resulting or not! It is exactly failure to handle such important personnel issues properly that can bring in a union in the first place.) If you have a grievance presented to you as a result of a termination and you are *wrong*, not only is it difficult to fit the employee back into the workforce, but people will never forgive you for the error. It is well worth being sure of your ground before action is taken. Hopefully done correctly, the case will never become a grievance, and if it does you will prevail.

The first step, of course is to know the union contract and to know established rules and procedures. Here is a little check list which should help in arriving at sound decisions in case of pending termination. Don't act until you are sure!

Are you sure you have all the facts? Have they been checked by someone other than the parties involved?

Did the employee know the rule or practice which was violated or at least should he or she have reasonably known it?

Does the management have a record of strict enforcement in cases of this kind? If not, was there a recent shop-committee warning or a well publicized campaign stating that management was going to "crackdown"?

In this instance was discipline applied reasonably in accord with the rule or with past practice? Are there specific provisions for immediate discharge spelled out in the rules such as striking a supervisor, drugs on the premises, drinking on the job, etc.,etc.?

Is this employee personally guilty or only guilty by association? Can guilt be proven by direct, factual evidence or is the evidence circumstantial?

Does the employee have a reasonable excuse for the infraction or infractions? Who asked about the excuse and checked it?

In cases where it is appropriate, has the employee been warned previously *in writing* for previous infractions and been given lesser penalties with the clear message that continued rule breaking would result in discharge? This is particularly important where the problem is failure to deliver the quality or quantity of work which is required. In other words firings for failure to do the job properly require good sound documentation and where the union is involved should have at least one clear record of warning having been given with the union representative present.

What is the employee's disciplinary record? What is his length of service?

Is some lesser penalty such as a "penalty lay-off" more appropriate?

Have the appropriate preliminary procedures been followed including notifying the union in accordance with established practice or as set out in the Collective Bargaining Agreement?

Is the rule which has been violated reasonable? Has it been applied fairly in this case? Does the punishment fit the crime? Are you, or the supervisor who is pressing for discharge, being level-headed and fair about the case?

Is this employee receiving the same treatment others have received in similar cases? (Note that in many Agreements an outside arbitrator is called for to settle this type of grievance and the parties must accept the arbitrator's decision.)

Discharge is often warranted, but it is a severe penalty that affects not only the employee himself but also any who are dependent on his or her earnings and may have far-reaching consequences. For instance in some states unemployment compensation is forfeited in cases of discharge for cause. You may also be asked for references when the employee applies for other employment and your answer may make the difference between the employee getting the job and not, etc. etc. On the other hand, when discharge is warranted, failure to act will affect the morale and action of the entire workforce. It only takes a couple of instances to ruin the standard of discipline and get *you* accused of favoritism!

Incidentally it is often easier to handle discipline in the union shop where the contract can be used to settle questions than it is in the non-union situation where "company policy" or "past practice" is the basis for discipline. Unless there is an excellent Personnel Practices Manual (these exist usually only in large organizations), determining just what "company policy" has been for instance may be pretty difficult!

STRIKE!

Now let's talk about the ultimate. A disagreement which leads to a strike is the ultimate in "Labor Trouble". As pointed out above, strikes usually result from disputes which affect groups of employees such as terms and conditions of employment, major contract negotiations, or organizing efforts. They result from a *failure* both in competence and in judgment on one side or the other of the bargaining table. While a strike may appear to be sudden and unexpected, it almost always results from an extended period of bad practices or from an outside force whose effect could have been predicted or anticipated, but more about that later.

As a general rule, all strikes last longer than anyone expects!! Once strikers "hit the bricks", there is a change in everyone's attitude, management and labor alike. Management tends to switch its energy to coping with customers, security of the physical facility, arranging for continuing operation to the extent possible, providing housing in the case of a hospital or a boarding school and such other pressing matters rather than simply trying to get the strikers back on the job. As a unit manager, you will be concerned with what can be done about keeping your portion of the operation going and will only get back to what you can do in resolving the dispute (if anything!) when you have done the best you can to cope with the disruption. The labor leaders on the other hand spend their energy on solidifying the strike position and ensuring that the members have plenty of excuses for "unity", getting picket lines and signs organized, making statements to the press, etc. etc. Remember they are politicians and have to rally their supporters. While management is plenty busy with its problems, on the labor side there is a kind of holiday atmosphere and the more boisterous members take over, especially on the picket line. All of a sudden a week has gone by. There is no paycheck and attitudes start to harden goaded on by the media getting involved and staging clips for the evening news or writing "personal interest" stories about how families are managing to get by. In due course strikes boil down to *raw power* and can get quite brutal, fast. This is when the "incidents" start and rocks get thrown through windows or sabotage occurs by those who believe this is the way to bring the corporation or institution to its knees. Strikes involving non-profit institutions and professional people can be just as brutal as those which are strictly factory based. Just think of the TV clips of striking teachers or hospital employees.

Here are a few observations about conditions during a strike that may be useful should you be involved in a strike situation.

Competitors will only give "pat-on-the-back" help. Even though your fight may be of great value to them in terms of establishing contract limits in your sector of the economy, your customers are fair game in a strike and your competitor is likely to be pointing out how unreliable you are as a source of supply or of service rather than pitching in to help you meet your customers' needs. It's part of the economic pressure a strike is meant to create.

Customers or clients are more helpful than competitors, but you have to level with them so they can make their plans to suffer as little damage as possible because of *your* strike. When you think a strike may be in the offing, be pessimistic with your customers, be sure they understand what might happen and do everything possible to cover their needs. If yours is an industrial operation putting inventory on consignment in their plant is a good idea so you don't have to move material through picket lines when the strike comes. If it is a service like an airline, have arrangements to offer other reservations or to be as helpful as possible to your clients. If your business is health care, take the initiative to call clients with appointments and offer alternatives. Don't "surprise" your customers with a strike!

In service businesses be ready to find your "good clients" honoring picket lines. Many people don't want to be exposed to taunts and possible violence even when they are not in sympathy with the strikers.

City and County law enforcement agencies are concerned and are usually co-operative in case of strike. They don't want any violence and realize that if violence occurs, they will be held partly responsible for not having done their job. But, lots of outside lights and a camera are more effective than the police in keeping violence down. After all, the police are part of the political scene as well. As they see it, you and the rest of the management may not even vote in their community and the strikers may be friends and relatives. Most police have their own union and sympathize with organization. Remember, too, federal labor law protects union officers from responsibility for violence in labor disputes.

In the case of a factory, production immediately before a strike is likely to be off-specification. Production during a strike whether by management or by non-strikers is likely to be of better quality than normal if for no other reason than people going "back to the book" in operating procedures.

Quick action is required to slow or to cancel deliveries of purchased raw materials and component parts especially where long-term contracts are involved. If nothing else, not having crews available to unload deliveries results in demurrage charges. Most suppliers will be reasonable and consider labor trouble as an "Act of God". After all, they want to continue doing business with your company. Service businesses must also stop deliveries of food and other supplies.

Don't use supervisors to transport non-strikers. This adds to resentment and can continue after the strike is over because those transported will be looked on as "favorites". Much better to pay for other transportation such as a pick-up bus or group taxi.

The stress. emotional impact and sheer physical exhaustion resulting from strike conditions is usually under-estimated. Not only are people doing jobs to which they are not accustomed, but they are working long hours under difficult circumstances. For many people it is rather like being under battle conditions. The long hours and perceived danger also has a devastating effect on family members especially if there are incidents of violence. There can be a lot of pressure from home in some instances and what may be exciting for you may be very hard for others to cope with.

Once they are on strike, there is no good way to communicate with employees. Letters, radio messages, advertisements are all immediately discounted by the union and in any case come under such severe legal restraints that they aren't convincing. Try reading some of the full page ads which are supposed to tell the company's side of a labor dispute and you will see what I mean. After the lawyers get through with them, it takes a lawyer to read it!

DON'T, REPEAT DON'T, get on any TV talk shows or do any taped interviews for TV. The latter are particularly bad because the clip which is aired is likely to be completely out of context and patched with scenes of marching strikers or other emotional stories about suffering families etc. The talk shows are bad because the interviewer just doesn't operate under the same rules you do and you have no control over what he is going to say. Labor disagreements are not settled in the press or by television; they are settled at the bargaining table. Like the TV interviewer and many politicians, the union representative has no qualms about making outrageous statements to the media about company actions whether true or not. Thus it's best not to get into a public debate with union representatives regardless of the forum. If you feel that public charges by the union must be answered, a simple denial is often best. You are better off saying to a reporter, "That's just not true. Have you been shown evidence you can trust not just somebody's assertion?" Rather than trying to go into a detailed defense or trying to convince a reporter that your position is right, throw the burden of proof back on the interviewer. "You wouldn't want to publish something that just isn't true?" Reporters hesitate to write something that "just isn't true". Don't try to justify a wage offer or to argue why the union's demand is too high. The proper answer to this type of question is, "That's up to the negotiating committee to work out."

Most local retail businessmen will show support for their striking customers rather than for management or the institution. In the case of strikes involving schools or hospitals, retailers do not want to antagonize parents or relatives of those affected by the loss of service.

Unionized labor is thoroughly indoctrinated with loyalty to their union. Loyalty to their employer is well down on the list partly because the media continues to play up the picture of "exploitation" by corporations and other institutions. Leaders of national unions are more interested in maintaining national patterns than in any local problem. When the VP from the International shows up, you can be sure his attitude is, "If this operation has to go out of business, other union members in other facilities will get the work. So if this corporation or institution can't meet our national pattern, it's better to have it out of the picture." The International has no problem with "restraint of trade".

Most workers think corporations earn fantastic profits, that all CEOs get outrageous salaries and all non-profit institutions are supported by very rich people. No amount of appeal on behalf of the stockholders means anything even when employees are stockholders. The only telling argument is proof that jobs will be lost if the organization is not competitive. Specific examples of failure to win orders or contracts and the number of jobs lost as a result of not having the business are good to publicize. Be sure to keep the workforce informed of "cause and effect" as you go along through the year, then they will believe you at negotiation time. Tell them of business lost as well as business won. You can't have good news all year long and then plead poverty at contract time. The same thinking applies to non-profit institutions. It does not help to talk all year about what a wonderful job is being done by the institution and its employees and then at contract time try to change the tune! Most complicated of all are the public employees such as teachers, city and town and state employees where negotiations are often carried on by committees of elected officials who may have no personal liability or stake in the outcome at all.

By and large politicians regardless of party affiliation (as contrasted to the police authorities) have little sympathy for management or for corporations. Politicians actually believe their own statements about corporations and other institutions exploiting their employees, and they also believe that management spends most of its time figuring out ways to avoid paying taxes or avoiding regulations. Even in strikes involving government activities with "No Strike" contracts, politicians will side with the strikers and worry about the consequences later. Strikers vote in elections! In practically every dispute you can depend on the politicians taking the side of the strikers and asking the company or institution to give in regardless of the facts or the economics. You can also expect a rash of complaints by the union to OSHA or the Labor Relations Board and to any other regulatory agency they can get into the act. Unfortunately, once started these actions usually go on way beyond the duration of the strike itself regardless of the merits. Unions are not known for their large campaign contributions because they love to give their members' money away and politicians are well aware of the clout which unions have at election time.

As negotiations continue, if you are involved and in a position to do so, in spite of all the extra work involved, keep the formal, written contract up-to-date so it can be signed the day agreement is reached. There is nothing worse than having to wait a week for the lawyers to complete their work on the formal contract only to have the union representatives say that what the lawyers have written is not what was agreed to. Delay means a chance for second thoughts. Remember, the union negotiators and officers are not businessmen and as politicians see nothing wrong with having "second thoughts", especially if they are being pressured by their members. It helps to remember that these people are union *representatives*, not executives. That doesn't mean they are stupid or just trouble-makers. Many professional union leaders are highly educated, very smart and certainly dedicated to their work. They deserve respect for what they are doing even if you don't agree with them, but like politicians they ultimately answer to the members whom they represent and can't agree to something which the members won't accept.

Bad feelings from a labor dispute actually disappear quite quickly especially if the first-line supervision takes a "business as usual" attitude putting the strike experience into history. It is important that the first line supervisors get the word that there are to be no recriminations. They should not moan about how tough it was working during the strike and they should not attempt to justify their own actions in carrying on the work of the unit. The less said, the better. Don't make a lot of statements about being "just one big happy family". No one will believe it and a strike costs the strikers economically for some time so they won't be too happy! Just get back on the job and get everything back to normal as soon as possible. Long strikes may well take years before the strikers are back even economically. A little arithmetic will prove that to you.

Working 50 weeks a year at 40 hours per week is 2000 hours. If off the job 6 weeks or 240 hours to get a 5% greater wage increase than would have been obtained without a strike, the employee needs 2.4 years before he or she is even on the wages lost during the strike.

YOUR ROLE IN AVOIDING LABOR TROUBLE

The key to avoiding strikes and serious labor trouble is to work at it all year around. It is said, **"A company or an institution gets the kind of union it deserves"** A regular program of talking with employees so they know the business climate and the competitive environment is an absolute must whether the organization is for or non-profit. But even more, one has to listen to what employees are saying and their grievances must be dealt with promptly. There is a great tendency during the year to tell employees only the rosy picture partly because of management's ego desire to appear successful and partly because one believes the employees are happier when they think the company or organization is doing well. You can't talk success all year and show up at the bargaining table claiming you can't afford to give a raise. That's *bad* management! Also vital is a regular program of working with the first level management, the foremen and unit leaders, to keep them informed and in the picture. If you are one of these first level people, you should keep alert to knowing what is going on so you can keep your people informed. You have great influence on employee attitudes and your actions may make the difference. The old "Bull of the Woods" type of supervisor still exists, but you don't want him in your shop! When the time comes for the union bargaining committee to take the new contract back to the membership, the trust from what you have done during the year may be as important in getting the contract ratified as what has been done at the bargaining table.

Another important ingredient in avoiding serious labor trouble is "appreciation" for the people making up the workforce. It may sound trite, but the Golden Rule is a great guide to employee relations. Included in appreciation is the recognition that the union representatives have a job to do and are proud of it. They should be talked to regularly and should be educated about the business or the institution so they understand some of the elements beyond the shop floor. To the extent possible they should have advance knowledge of events that may affect the workforce and should be listened to in planning how to deal with lay-offs or other changes that affect the people. This doesn't mean you can shift responsibility to the union reps, but it does mean you can be sure they understand the facts about what is going on so they can stop rumors and misinformation.

So long as there are two sides to the bargaining table, there will be "labor trouble". The task of the good manager is to minimize the effect of any disagreements and to keep his work force producing. In this regard, the over-all labor climate in any organization is made up of the sum total of every interaction between management and labor or between supervisor and someone being supervised. The president of the company may be the most enlightened executive in the world with regard to labor relations and may be an absolute genius in dealing with those persons he supervises, but if the message and the execution doesn't go through all levels right to the factory floor, labor relations problems will result. The dean of a school may be an absolute genius in dealing with alumni, but if he or she is not responsive to the inside staff at all levels, difficulty is sure to follow. The hospital administrator may be outstanding in dealing with the individual professional, but if the general staff is not kept in the picture, it is a formula for difficulty. Almost always labor problems come from poor practices at the lowest levels of supervision rather than from the top. This means that regardless of where *you* fall in the organization, what you do can make a difference. Very few employees want a union just to get more money. When the employees can't find out what is going on that affects them or when employees go to their supervisors with questions and the reply is, "I'm busy and can't waste time with your problems." or the equivalent, those employees will look to a union representative in order to get the power of the group action. It is up to you by your actions to choose with whom you would rather deal!

CHAPTER 15

HANDLING THE MEDIA

You may think that you will never come in contact with "The Media" and therefore this chapter is not for you. Not true! No matter where you are in the organization, you may be called upon to deal with the media in some form or the other. The need usually comes when some out-of-the-ordinary event has occurred like a fire or a strike or an accident. Reporters or a TV crew arrive and *you* are the only one available! There are a few basic rules which will get you through the ordeal unscathed.

The first thing to keep in mind is that the reporters and the TV crews don't care about *your* problems. They have been sent out to get a story and to meet a deadline. They are experts at controlling you and controlling the story. There is a certain awe about having a microphone thrust in your face or having a reporter, pad in hand, earnestly asking questions. You *must not* let them keep you from doing what you should do first. Take care of whatever the emergency may be and talk to the media afterward. Don't be polite about this. Just keep in mind that the media don't care what happens to you or to the victim or to your reputation or anything else. **Don't make off-hand comments just because a microphone is thrust in your face and cameras are grinding.** There is no reason to let a reporter or TV crew come on your private property and add to the

problems you are already facing.(Incidentally the company or institution will be just as liable for any accident that occurs to a reporter
or TV crew that you have allowed on the property as it would be for
any other private citizen. Just because they have a press pass does-
n't make them any less likely to get hurt if they are where they
should not be.) Keep them under control and be sure the gate watch-
men know that the "press" has no privilege to come on the property just because they are the press.

Since your best policy is to keep the reporters and TV crews in the
street until you are ready to talk with them, the story they will be picking up is from whoever is available: firemen, EMT personnel, neigh-
bors, taxi drivers etc. You have all had the experience of seeing the
man on the street being interviewed about some major event like the
bombing of the Word Trade Center just because that person was readily available. This story is most likely to be a slanted story unfavorable
to your organization so as soon as possible a spokesman should get to
the media. If it can be arranged, get the reporters and TV crews away
from the scene of the action into some location where the briefing can
take place calmly. No matter what *you* say, the surroundings will
affect the way the story looks and sounds. Just think of some of the TV
coverage you have seen of ordinary accidents and the camera focus on
hysterical people rather than some responsible official. Get to a conference room or to a quiet place in the warehouse or to a garage where
everything is under control and the spokesperson can concentrate on
the story without distractions. Also getting away from the scene
allows necessary work there to go on undisturbed.

If you are to be the spokesperson, it is always a good idea to start
with a written statement. If at all possible, take a moment before
meeting with the media to jot down what you are going to tell them
and insist that you read your statement first. When the press conference starts after a calamity has taken place, there will be a barrage
of questions—probably shouted! Just say, "I will answer all your
questions in a moment, but please quiet down while I read this
statement that tells you what happened". The statement should be

brief and factual covering what happened, who got injured, any damage to the neighborhood and where the situation stands at the moment. Again, don't let reporters firing questions control the interview. If you don't know what happened, say so. "We really are not sure what happened and won't know until the fire marshal investigates." or "We can't tell exactly what happened until we are able to talk with the victim." The reason why persons who appear before Congressional Committees read a prepared statement before they testify is to get the story they want to have heard on the record before the committee takes control. You should do the same thing in any dealings with the media.

In the interview, don't speculate and don't answer hypothetical questions. As a reasonable person, you are likely to answer a question like, "If the fire had gotten to the big storage tank in the back yard, isn't it possible it would have exploded?" by saying something like, "Unlikely, but yes, that would be possible." only to find the headline reading, "Company spokesman says big storage tank could have exploded!" Or worse still with the TV technique of showing only those portions of an answer that suits their purpose, the question will be posed and only that bit of your answer that says, "Yes, that would be possible." will come out.

Some questions should not be answered at all. If you have recognized a reporter and do not wish to answer the question, either say something like, "That is a good question, but the information is confidential at this time." or you can say, "That is a good question." and proceed to change the subject making some statement you wish to get on the record. There is no rule that says one must answer every question a reporter asks. For their part remember that the reporter will choose to print or to show only a fraction of any interview and you should feel you have the same right to "edit" what you say as they have to edit what you say. This is not to infer that you should fabricate any answers. Anything you say should be completely factual, but it does not have to be everything you know.

Up to this point we have been dealing with the unforeseen situation where preparation is minimal at best. If the organization is large enough to have a specific person responsible for public relations, even in an emergency situation it is always best to leave as much of the talking as possible to that person who will have thought ahead of time about handling this kind of event and will probably already have a working understanding with the reporters. Know how to get in touch with the PR person if your job could possibly result in a "media event".

A completely different set of circumstances surrounds the planned interview on a subject for which you have been chosen as one of the interviewees. In this case the reporter will usually be accompanied by your PR person or by the person who arranged the interview. If possible, have the reporter agree at the outset to allow you to check the resulting piece "to be sure the facts are correct." No reporter will, or should, let his work be edited to shape the story, but facts are facts and you have the responsibility to see they are being reported accurately. The reader is more likely to think that you didn't know what you were doing than that the reporter got it wrong.

In every case have a tape recorder running during the entire interview so there is a record of precisely what was said. It is usual for the reporter to have his own recorder, but that is not enough. You should have *your own* recorder. Even with a recorder, it is a good idea to have another person present during the interview, usually your PR representative if one exists. In the chapter on "How to Make People Understand What You Say" we point out that every institution has a language of its own, terms which have a particular meaning to the organization. One of the reasons for the recorder is to avoid mistakes made when you use terms the reporter does not understand or even more when the reporter deliberately leaves out some qualifying remark when doing his or her piece. If you have to ask for a retraction, the recorded interview is invaluable.

The rules for the planned interview are about the same as for the emergency one. If you know the subject and want to have a prepared statement, it is usually sufficient just to give it to the reporter with the words, "Here is something I have written up on the subject which may be useful to you." When the subject involves lots of facts and figures, the prepared statement is particularly important because reporters in general have a very poor grasp of figures. They just don't think that way! Think how many times you have seen *millions* and *billions* mixed up in press reports. In the trade the prepared material is called a "Press Kit".

Next in importance is to listen carefully to the reporter's question—all of it! If you answer the question before the reporter has finished asking it, you may be answering the wrong question and confusing the reporter. Take your time. The reporter is not nearly so knowledgeable about the subject as you are. If you sense the reporter really hasn't understood what you said or hasn't grasped the thought, either re-phrase your answer or ask the reporter, "Just to be sure we understand each other would you please tell me what I just said means to you?" Likewise if you don't understand a question, don't hesitate to ask that it be repeated or say something like, "If I understood your question, it was..." and repeat the question in your own words. Again, when fig-ures are involved, try to put them in context, something like, "We make 2,000 tons a day. That's *four* million pounds, you know." or "That is enough policies to have one for every person in Chicago."

Don't try to be a hero and don't try to show how smart you are or how much you know. Just stick to the facts and the reporter's ques-tions. There is no need to volunteer information that isn't asked for and no need to tell the reporter he or she isn't asking the right ques-tions. The exception to this rule is when the reporter has a total mis-understanding of the subject or the situation and is working from a completely improper or biased position. When this occurs, it is well to stop and take the time to reach an understanding on the ground rules. How one goes about this depends on the circumstances. Reporters do not necessarily have the business point of view and that is their prerogative, but they do not have the right to ignore the facts or even worse, create their own. Words like, "It seems to me that the situation we are discussing is basically different from what you think it is and before we go any further with this interview we should get on the same wave-length." will give you a chance to clear up the discrepancy or misunderstanding by getting the facts on the table. If the reporter already has his mind made up and you don't like his positions, it is probably best to conclude the interview as quickly and as politely as possible.

It is very tricky to talk to a reporter "off the record". Unless you are very sure of your ground it is best to keep everything "on the record" and just limit what you tell the reporter. If you want to take the chance of saying something you don't want your name associated with, it's best to use words along the following line, "What I am about to tell you is off-the record. Do you want to hear it on that basis? I can tell you that if I see anything in print attributed to our organization or to me, I will deny the whole thing." This is tricky territory and best left to the experts. Even they don't do it very well most of the time!

Just one more word about "Off the Record". Reputable reporters will honor an agreement about statements that are "Off the Record", but as pointed out above, this is a particularly tricky aspect of dealing with the media. There is always the gray area between what has been said on the record and what was off the record and this borderline area can easily lead to misunderstanding. Almost as important is the impression made with the reporter who must either feel that there is even more to the story which is not being revealed or must believe that you don't have the courage to state your position openly. There is a growing body of reporting that depends on "not for attribution" or the source who speaks "on the condition of anonymity". The danger in all this is the reporter does not have to be careful about keeping his own personal bias out of the story. Since no one is named as responsible for the content of the story, the reporter can put in almost anything he or she wants to. The best position is to say nothing "Off the Record".

In the normal circumstances as the interview concludes, it is a good idea to summarize the entire subject. To do this properly means you should have been jotting down notes as the interview goes along so you will remember all the points made as the interview developed. Urge the reporter to call you as he or she works up the story and runs into further questions or finds he is not sure of what his notes mean. As pointed out above, the best situation is to be able to look at the story before it is published, "To check the facts." Most reporters try to do a responsible job and usually welcome the opportunity to be accurate in their stories. If you have taken the chance with an "off the record" comment, be sure that it doesn't appear in the resulting story in such a way that it can be attributed to you.

Once the story has been published, there is little one can do about it if the story is unfavorable. In cases of outright error, publications will often print a correction in small type on some inside page or will publish a "Letter to the Editor", but the effect is minimal. TV stations usually won't even go that far unless the error is so gross as to affect their reputation. The best policy is to get the story right in the first place.

In summary, dealing with the media is not to be taken lightly. The image and the public record which is created is something that is not easy to change once established and should be undertaken with appropriate care. On the other hand the time may well come when you are faced with being a spokesperson. Having thought about the possibility ahead of time is half the battle!

CHAPTER 16

THE COMPUTER IN YOUR LIFE

One of the great technical advances in the last half of the 20th Century was the advent of "data processing". In the years since 1980, the revolution became a wild-fire swept by the low cost and ready availability of the desk-top personal computer, the ubiquitous PC, and now its cousins the "Notebook" and the "Palm Pilot" plus Apple's "Mac", linux, unix and all the rest. The purpose of this chapter is to put the world of computers and data processing into perspective as it relates to the function of the supervisor/manager. Exciting as this revolution may be, it is important to have a clear understanding of the manager's use of the tool because, after all, the computer is just one more tool in the manager's "bag of tricks".

First, let's emphasize the difference between the manager and the technical professional since for the latter the computer has become almost indispensable because of its manipulative power and its ability to access data bases. One can hardly imagine a chemist or a financial analyst or a librarian working without the capability of a computer. Secondly, there are many persons who have to know all about computers and programming because that is their job just as automotive engineers and automobile repairmen must know all about the workings of an automobile. As a *manager/supervisor* you have completely different needs. Certainly you need know no more about the inside of the computer than you know about the automobile in which you commute to work. Like the automobile, you must be comfortable with what computers have to offer. To use them as a manager you do need a clear picture of the limitations of these wonderful devices when it comes to the task of the manager. Computers can be great aids to effectiveness, but they can be great time-wasters if the manager doesn't use them properly. Let's go over the subject slowly!

There are two principles to be kept in mind when dealing with computers or computer applications:

> The computer will only do what it has been told or "programmed" to do.

> The computer can only work with the information or data it has been given.

It should be apparent that there is plenty of room for error in just these two simple statements. Thus the absolute guiding principle in dealing with computers is:

> Just because the computer says it's so, doesn't make it so. Always test any computer statement to see if it makes sense. Take a "squint" before accepting the result or output.

This is the same rule which is applied to statements which come from accounting or from financial analysis or from a production report. Just because the information is on an official form or expressed in numbers or on a computer screen or on a print-out doesn't make it so!

Now let's move along to see what a computer can do and how it should be used. This is pretty basic stuff, but it won't hurt even the accomplished computer user to review a few fundamentals. One can classify the work a computer can do in the following manner:

It can store, sort and retrieve information as a kind of electronic file clerk. The library catalog is a good example.

It can perform standardized repetitive operations such as making out paychecks, mailing labels, tax returns, maintaining inventory records, developing accounting reports, etc. etc.

It can manipulate large amounts of data with great speed, performing extensive calculations rapidly and at low cost. The actual calculations are done with a high degree of accuracy exactly as specified. The results, however, are only as valid as the data which were input.

It can, to the extent a system can be characterized, simulate what happens in the system when conditions change. This ability translates into the use of computers to control chemical processes or machine tools, to pilot aircraft, to simulate business situations or even to simulate the behavior of the economy! It has significant use in design calculation, prediction of chemical structures, analysis of tax returns and a whole host of similar tasks where the rules and limits can be specified.

It can act as a "storage bank" where information is gathered from outside sources and kept available as for example by "e-mail". It can also be the access point to outside information on the "web" through a variety of services as diverse as stock market quotations to personal bulletin boards. The Internet network is the ultimate example of this access power. The computer also gives one the ability to use the work of others by the purchase of disks, especially the CD ROM type, which can contain everything from the contents of an encyclopedia to video games to movies; the so-called multi-media revolution.

It can make exactly the same information available to a number of outlets or it can instantly transmit data or instructions from one computer to another of which e-mail is again an example.

It is the basis for the "Desktop Publishing" phenomenon which is a sophisticated form of data manipulation involving fonts and images.

Again, it should be apparent that in each of these applications the result is only as good as the original analysis on which the "program" is based and only as good as the data on which the computer acts, which it collects, or with which it is supplied. (Which incidentally is one of the faults of a computer. It can not discriminate based on the quality of the figures or other information with which it works. All figures and all words look the same to a computer regardless of their inherent validity.) The computer does not have "intellect" in the accepted sense of the word. What actually happens is a programmer tries to describe a system and to give instructions to the computer (a *program*), in a language which the computer can use, about what to expect in the way of in-puts and what the proper response to each in-put is. Actual examples are then taken and the program is adjusted, or "de-bugged", until the responses from the computer are always the desired ones. It should be clear that programs are not always perfect because the programmer has not anticipated and allowed for every situation which might develop. Even the computer may be defeated by the grand-master chess player!

"No program is completely fool-proof."

It should be equally clear that some tasks which are done in exactly the same way each time, e.g. writing a check, are quite simple to program and the action is highly reliable. On the other hand, we have all had experience with mailing lists where the computer quite accurately generates labels for the same address differing only by a single initial or the use of a given name rather than an initial thus resulting in several copies of the same catalog to what is in fact the same person. Until someone inspects the list and makes some judgement as to the duplication or until another program is used which screens and compares *every* element of the address to eliminate duplication, the computer will continue to do as it has been told and will keep sending extra copies.

Now let's describe the "personality" of a computer since many people have come to think of computers as almost human.

It works extremely rapidly, is completely tolerant of monotony, never gets tired although very occasionally it gets "sick". All computers experience short-term problems as the result of "crashes" or "freezes" and long term problems caused by the failure of one of the components. All are subject to viruses or glitches in programs. Backing up the computer's memory should be a required routine!

It doesn't make mistakes like errors in addition, putting a properly identified record in the wrong file or spilling the coffee.

It will take orders from anyone who can identify himself properly and who can get access to the processor. It doesn't argue back unless specifically instructed otherwise (as for instance when one tries to use an improper command) and it treats all persons exactly alike showing no prejudice.

The computer has no imagination and no ability to improvise on instructions it has been given. Every detail has to be thought through by someone else and "explained" to the computer. It will believe anything it is told and will attempt to do anything it is told to do within its capabilities.

It has no morality. It has no sense of purpose of its own. By themselves, computers are neither good nor evil.

Behind every computer, behind every program, behind every information disk are one or more humans and it is they who are responsible in an ethical sense for whatever the computer does or reports.

THE COMPUTER AND MANAGEMENT

Now to look at its relationship to the manager's tasks, let's re-state the functions a computer can perform and which underlie its usefulness.

It can store large quantities of data (or, if you will, information) for manipulation. Some of this information may be instructions for the computer telling it how to respond to outside inputs or how to manipulate the information it has available.

It can accept input of new data and it can output data which it has stored or manipulated (processed) including messages received by telephone or by other message networks.

It can move data around in its storage or "memory" without changing its "value" or form, e.g. it can take a sentence from one page and move it to another without changing any of the letters or it can move a number from one place to another without changing its value.

It can perform calculations using mathematical techniques and it can "count", compare and identify.

It can control the sequence of instructions which it follows, i.e. on command it can jump from one point in a series of instructions to another point and return if necessary.

Everything a computer does is some variation or combination of the essential elements listed above. The computer has been hailed as the great leap forward in modern management and the answer to a multitude of problems. There is no doubt that a computer can be a useful management tool, but like all powerful phenomena it has to be controlled so it doesn't get out of hand. Because a computer works at such blinding speed and at such relatively low cost compared to doing a job manually, there is a great tendency to do by computer many things which really were better left undone! It's a little like buying the fur coat one doesn't need and rarely would use just because it's on sale. Thus the first step in the effective management use of computers is to decide what should be done using computer power.

In many institutions computers are well established as a management tool based on the data processing capability from a start made usually just after WWII when the punch card systems came into common use. Because in most organizations this new technique was first picked up by the financial types, for many years use of the computer was dominated by the needs and wishes of financial services and the computer professionals tended to report to, and to have their priorities set by, the financial services management. Although the use of computers has become more widespread as hardware costs have plummeted and the so-called personal computer has become commonplace, financial services or the accounting departments in many organizations still control access to much of the data the manager finds most useful and they are still considered to be the "experts". (I don't speak here of the technical and research applications of the computer mainly as a data reservoir, calculator or simulator in laboratories and engineering establishments or of the data banks of forms and decisions used in law offices and other such uses. As explained at the beginning of this chapter, this is a category unto itself). The manager should realize that the financial "types" may not have the expertise they claim to have because their approach is quite limited. Even in the small organization, it is usually the financial types who are most intimately involved with computers. What this means to the non-financial manager is he or she can expect to be able to obtain reports on, or analysis of, standard accounting data or on other data routinely used by financial services personnel, but once outside this area it may not be so simple. I'm not talking about word processing or other universal applications of computer power for which generalized, public programs are available, but rather the application of the computer to specialized problems unique or nearly so to the business or institution and to the specific situation which the manager faces. Usually, however, the problem for a manager is to avoid being overwhelmed by the sheer volume of statistics and words which a computer can generate.

For example, the simple request, "I would like to see a monthly report of sales by product." in the hands of the computer specialist can easily become a monthly report of sales by product, sales by customer, products by customer, sales by salesman, products by salesman, sales by state, products by state, sales by city, products by city, sales by zip code, etc. etc. as the computer specialist tries to prove how smart he is and how versatile the machine. While all this information may be useful at one time or another, it certainly isn't needed as a management tool all the time, and in large measure represents a waste of computer time and, more importantly, of your time. (After the first month you probably will only look at the one variation that is most useful to you and throw the rest in the wastepaper basket!) Thus an important rule in dealing with the computer wizards (They are found under different names in different organizations: Financial Services, Management Services: Data Processing: Computer Sciences, Whatever!) is to have a meeting of the minds on *exactly* what it is that you need for your purposes and what you intend to do with the output.

Next, computers are like a fascinating toy or puzzle and there is a great tendency for the manager to spend more time "playing" at his computer terminal than is warranted. In today's computer world the manager, and for that matter many professionals like lawyers or doctors, should know how to use and should be comfortable with a computer, but each must discipline himself to use it as an assistant for what it can do for him and not as a toy. Even the most mundane programs now have so many "bells and whistles" that trying to be proficient is a big job. As this chapter is written, Borland Office comes with 11 manuals, Lotus SmartSuite comes with 13 and Microsoft Office Professional with 10! Each of these combinations is supposed to be just the basic tools required in a modern office. Back to the analogy of the automobile, in this automotive age a person is at a serious disadvantage in not knowing how and not being licensed to drive, but once the skill has been acquired and the license won, the urge to joy-ride or otherwise use an auto when not appropriate has to be controlled. Certainly, while he is on the job, the manager should not be spending his time becoming a computer expert or surfing the web to see what is new.

Often it is better to let someone else do the computer work you have defined and to have that person just bring you the results unless your immediate interaction with the output is important as in a "what if" analysis. Certainly you should let the experts do whatever programming has to be done including de-bugging. Avoid doing anything an intelligent assistant can do which translates to, "Put the terminal on your associates desk, not on yours." This probably isn't actually practical because at times you will want immediate access to what the unit can do for you, but it is very easy to get fascinated with the computer and to spend too much time fooling with it. As a manager, you are supposed to be getting results from other people and not doing the job yourself! In this regard it may be useful to think of the computer as another very proficient person from whom you want results with a minimum input of your own time.

One of the characteristics of both the telephone and computer mail is a tendency to dominate time. Legend has it that Alexander Graham Bell once said he'd never have a telephone in the house. While e-mail and other forms of bulletin board and Fax transmission services are great in their immediacy, they have no sense of priority and you must supply that ingredient. Just as you may decide not to answer the phone because there are more important things to do, you should decide to leave e-mail until working with it is appropriate. There are programs now which have rules built into them such as "Notify me if I receive a message from the boss." and the system checks the sender name to see. Other messages can just be filed to be brought up later like regular mail. Managing is *not* "answering the mail".

While on the subject, *be cautious* with messages you send by e-mail. It is so easy to dash off a message especially when you are agitated or angry, but once you hit the SEND button, there is no way to reconsider. The very characteristics which make e-mail so useful also make it potentially dangerous. In a face-to-face or phone conversation, you choose words with care and watch for reaction. You remember the social conventions and work around difficult situations. There is something about e-mail that makes one forget the niceties and behave in a different way from normal. Remember also as you compose your message that it may well be seen by someone other than the addressee. (Who knows what route an Internet message has traveled!) Many institutions routinely back-up messages routed over internal e-mail systems for future reference. Play it safe: always assume someone besides the addressee will be seeing your messages. Don't put anything in an e-mail or use offensive words or expressions you would not use in a face-to-face conversation or that you would not want anyone except the addressee to see. Charges of sexual harassment, discrimination and wrongful termination have all been upheld based on e-mail records. The breezy style is fun and e-mail can be a great way to be in instant communication with colleagues, but THINK before you SEND. The same caution goes for anything which is stored in computer memory. Anything which can be recovered is potentially public knowledge.

USING UNIQUE COMPUTER PROGRAMS

When you propose to bring computer power to bear on a unique situation where some non-standard program has to be developed, be prepared for the whole procedure to take longer than first estimates to be more complex than expected, and to cost much more than expected. As I write this, Harvard University is implementing a new system for which early estimates were $20 million for the whole job. After four years of work characterized by being "plagued by escalating costs, delays in implementation and slow system performance", the cost is now estimated at $100 million. To be sure Harvard is a large and complex institution with some 4,000 divisions, but on a smaller scale, its experience applies to everyone. In this regard, know what applicable programs may already be available and *listen to the experts.* It may seem simple to you, but they know and appreciate the infinite detail involved in every application program. In fact as in the Harvard case, even the experts tend to believe they can develop programs for non-standard applications with less time and effort than the work will actually take. (Think of the new Denver International airport and its computer controlled baggage handling system which took months to straighten out!) If what you want to do can't be handled by a tested program already in existence, stop and reconsider whether you really need the power of the computer.

> Will the resulting program be used many times, i.e. is this a mass production type use with long enough life to justify the effort and cost?
>
> Are the procedures involved fully understood and exceptions either limited in number or limited to a few categories that can be defined?
>
> Are peak workloads involved where people just can't get the job done and/or is extremely rapid response required?
>
> Can choices be made based on defined rules with no intuitive judgement or "taste" involved?
>
> Are the data to be used by many different people or for many different uses where consistency is important?
>
> If the program is to be marketed, is there really a market sufficient to repay the costs of development and are you willing to have others learn the methodology?

While these conditions are largely self-explanatory, a few examples may help in thinking about them. Except when a tested program is already available, the work required to set up and de-bug a computer program is probably more than the work required to simply handle the application manually *unless* the program will be used many times. Repetition shows up in many ways, but it is always present in a proper computer application. Even when you use a standard program for a single application, the only reason why the program exists for your use is because many people are repeatedly using it somewhere else. Microsoft is said to have spent more than $60 million developing its *Access* database program. It is available at a list price of $495 only because millions will be sold and used.

As far as having the procedures involved fully understood, if you don't know what you want to do, the computer is of no use. Very often when you think that the procedures are well understood, after the analysis required to write a proper program, you will find that the procedures are *not* understood. This may be one of the truly beneficial fall-outs of trying to develop a computer application. If the circumstances are such that it is "the exceptions which prove the rule", a computer can handle such a system only if the exceptions fall into well-defined classes for the handling of which the computer can be given appropriate and specific instructions. Computers have never been able to do precise, long-range weather forecasting in spite of their ability to compare vast numbers of patterns because there are too many exceptional circumstances involved whose effects cannot be specified. Computers do a great job of constructing fancy maps and showing movement of past weather patterns, but when it comes down to predicting what the local weather will be tomorrow, computers are no better than the old sailor!

The prime example of peak work loads and rapid response time is the airline reservation system. Only a centralized data bank instantly accessible allows the airline to sell tickets up to flight departure time and still keep control including just how much over-booking to permit! For the ordinary manager the *cost* of such flexibility has to be weighed against the advantages. There is no sense computerizing inventory if one can simply shout to the back of the store and get the necessary answer. On the other hand if your unit is just one of many and centralized buying is supplying your needs, then having all the data from many locations transmitted to a central processor is the way to go. Remember also that the data on which the computer relies has to be constantly up-dated if it is to be of any value and this function, too, is part of the cost.

In the usual business situation the test as to whether to computerize a function or not (in addition to the requirement for repetition) rests on what decisions or choices have to be made as part of the routine of the function. A computer makes choices or decisions by comparing or matching alternatives with well-defined parameters. Keep in mind a computer has no imagination and no ability to improvise on the instructions it has been given. If the personal element is important in a function, the computer is limited in its application. A good example is the personal touch required in most sales situations. A computer can tell that a certain item is not in stock, it can list whatever substitutes are available in inventory, but it cannot sooth an irate customer. In fact it is that exact impersonal nature of the computer which makes the customer irate when told a problem is "the computer's fault". What one wants from a doctor is his sympathetic, experienced evaluation of the state of one's health, not the computer print-out of an automated blood test with the normal limits marked. Computers are often wrong when asked to deal with political situations and are hopeless when it comes to making artistic determinations. Would a computer ever have chosen the Mona Lisa?? A computer can maintain a list of titles in the library, but cannot judge the relative quality of the various authors.

The power of the computer is certainly of great help in coping with the complexities of modern institutions and with the rate of change in today's world, but computers are not human, let alone super-human, and must be thought of and controlled as tools to be used in those situations and applications where using the power is cost-effective and appropriate. Where the human qualities of insight, intuition, judgement, sympathy or morality are important, the computer is of little help and it is the exercise of just these qualities which make up a large part of the manager's job. The manager can never afford to let a computer substitute for good sense, and he or she must avoid being buried in computer-generated information or overwhelmed by the time spent using the unit. Be very wary of the statement, "We'll just computerize this operation and your troubles will be over." And again, always take a "squint" at the work product of the computer to be sure *your* good sense tells you that the computer has got it right.

NET-NET

As this is written, the new fad is to be an e-manager. Perhaps the main lesson to be learned from the computer revolution as it affects the manager's job is that the most important of all computer in-puts are the human beings who are involved. Other chapters in this book are devoted to how the manager makes the most of these human resources. It is up to the manager to see that computer power maximizes what his people are capable of and that the use of computers helps to solve problems rather than add to them.

Part III

YOUR CAREER

CHAPTER 17

A LITTLE CAREER PLANNING

There are really three factors which have substantial impact on your career. Strange as it may seem, the first and probably most important is to pick a company or institution where the corporate culture suits your own style. More about this in a moment. Second, to the extent you are able, you must get the best possible people working around or for you. Good managers pick good associates. "Birds of a feather flock together." And finally, you must always be preparing yourself to be ready for the chance when it comes.

Let's talk about that last one first. As Edward R. Telling, former Chairman of Sears, Roebuck & Co., said in an interview given to the *The Wall Street Journal* in August of 1984,

> "If lightning should strike and you haven't prepared yourself...and if you haven't taken the trouble to know your mind and what you plan to do, then God help you. But I don't think the chairmanship should be anyone's goal, because it's chance that puts you in the position when you get right down to it. You have to be lucky enough to be the right age when the job opens. And there may be many people that are just as qualified as yourself

to fill the job. You still might not be tapped. I didn't expect
to be picked as chairman."

Talk to almost anyone whom you consider successful and they will
tell you if they are being honest about it that chance has played a large
part in their success. They will also tell you that they had worked hard
at being ready for the chance when it did come! I'm not talking about
jumping from entry level positions to chairman. The position you
want to prepare yourself for is the next one (or two) up the ladder (or
laterally if that is where the action is!) following the career path you
have chosen. Later in this section and in Chapter 19 you will find some
ideas about how to be ready when the opportunity comes.

Now let's go back to talk about corporate culture and its importance
to your career. Some organizations are highly structured, the Catholic
Church, the military, General Motors or A..T.&T. for example. Other
organizations seem almost amoeba-like in their lack of structure. This
is especially true in the smaller company where the CEO *is* the structure and everyone reports to him and does whatever has to be done,
or in the small, high-tech company where a group of dedicated people
are sort of gathered in a loose association or in the small museum with
eight or ten employees. Some organizations are highly "figure-orient-
ed" and everything has to be reduced to numbers whether appropriate or not. Other organizations are "cults" where everyone must play
golf or have a personal computer or spend summers in Nantucket. The
latter type is found most often in service organizations such as adver-
tising agencies, management consultants or software developers. No
need to go on. You have the idea.

JOB INTERVIEWS

A "Society", and all organizations or institutions *are* societies, has a
way of ejecting members that do not conform to its culture. It is therefore **very important** as you start your career, or as you change jobs,
that you choose a job situation in a company that has a culture with

which you are comfortable and compatible. You have a good opportunity to judge what a company is like when you interview for a job. If you are already on the job, I hope what follows will help you to understand the nature of the company you are in.

When you interview for a job, remember, any eventual position is much more important to you than it is to the person offering employment. Ask plenty of questions about the nature of the company and about the "cultural" things which are important in the company life. There is a classic *New Yorker* magazine cartoon which shows a prospective associate being conducted down the magnificent main corridor of a law firm by what is obviously a senior partner. From behind a half-opened door an unshaven, haggard, young face peers out and says in a hoarse whisper, "For God's sake, don't join this firm." The culture in that firm was far different from the appearances!

Very often the more senior people whom you may see in the interview process will be eager to tell you about the firm's culture. It is important to them since they helped create it.

For example:

"We all start work early around here. I'm always in by 7:30."

"Everybody is on the road in this company. Why, I was out of the office over half the time last year."

"The boss expects to see everyone in here on Saturday morning. It's so quiet we get a lot done!"

"We all do our bit for the community. Everyone is on some town committee or other."

"There are no organization charts around here except the one the boss keeps in his head."

"We all take part in the cultural activities around town. It is important to this institution

I don't have to go on. This is the kind of information *you* want to get out of an interview regardless of the kind of institution it may be. Don't worry too much about the details of the pension plan; you won't last until retirement if you choose the wrong culture. You know what kind of a person you are. If you are uncomfortable in an unstructured situation where you aren't just sure what your job is and where your responsibility stops, don't join up with an organization where this is the norm. Look instead for one with policy manuals, organization charts and position descriptions. On the other hand, if you are the kind of person who strikes out to get the job done regardless of whose responsibility it is, or if you suffer under spelled-out constraints and well-defined controls, then look for a situation where unstructured action is the order of the day. You probably won't find it in a government office. Don't take a position with the idea that the company culture won't apply to you or that somehow you will change things. I can guarantee that the organization or company will survive, but *you won't!*

Here are a few questions or statements that will help you decide something about yourself. Score each item from 1 to 10 with 1 being **not** important to your way of thinking and 10 being **very** important. If your score is over 40, you should be looking to work in a fairly structured and organized situation.

I like to know exactly what I am supposed to do and when I am supposed to do it.

Anyone who can't get his work done in 8 hours isn't organized.

Every organization should have a Policy Book one can turn to and find out what to do.

People should stick to the chain of command. I don't like anyone else telling my people what to do and I want only my own boss telling me what to do.

Facts and figures tell it all! I don't want to hear opinions. No adjectives, please!

You have to listen to the lawyers and the accountants before you try to do anything.

Finally, the quality of the people in the organization tells you a great deal about whether you will do well. I'm not talking about social quality; I'm talking about competence. One important part of the interview ordeal is the opportunity you have to judge the people who do the interviewing and those you meet around the company. Make a judgment on each one. You should expect that the clerk in the Personnel Department will not be of the same quality as the Vice President, *but* as clerks go, what do you think of his performance? How about the other people? Are they sharp, informed, intelligent? What is the ambience around the office? This is a two-way street and you should be as intent on forming a judgment about people with whom you may be working as your potential employer is in making a judgment about you. These are the people who will determine just how successful you are once you join their team.

PRESENTING YOURSELF

Listen! Your background has probably already been put into the hands of your interviewer. He or she usually has some definite approach to the interview process and your job is to make as good use of the time as possible. That means satisfying the interviewer's questions as succinctly and as briefly as possible. First you must listen to the question so your answer is responsive, but to be brief means that you should have done some preparation before the interview. Write out a summary of your work experience and education *with dates*. If some outside interests apply to the position, include them as well. Have a complete outline or description of your present job and what it entails. Titles are not enough and mean different things in different organizations. Finally, know why you are interested in the position for which you are being interviewed. Don't talk too much. If the interviewer wants to know more, let that person ask the question. More interviews have gone wrong because the person being interviewed couldn't stop talking than for almost any other reason.

Know ahead of time as much as you can about the company or institution for which you are being interviewed. Most large companies or non-profit institutions already have a well established reputation. It is worth doing your homework and reading up on just what that reputation is. Business magazines, annual reports and brokerage reports are good sources of information on corporations. Appropriate publications will deal with other institutions. Often there are national rankings developed for such institutions as universities or law schools. For the small company, particularly if it is privately held, you may have to rely on what the local people have to say about it. Finding out may be as basic as dropping in to the local diner for a cup of coffee and just asking the question, "Tell me about the X company? What kind of people are they?" It may sound like a waste of time, but it is *your* life that is in question.

ON THE JOB

Once you are on the job, it's up to you to get ahead. One of the great errors made by employees is to expect that "the company" is responsible for the training and the development of its personnel. Now it is true that any institution in its own selfish interest wants each employee to advance as far in the organization as possible, *but* it has no responsibility for any specific individual's success. It is the *individual* who is responsible for looking out for himself or herself. In fact no training or development program succeeds when the individuals involved are not self-motivated. Take advantage of any opportunities offered by the company to further your development and look on these opportunities as being a compliment, but don't depend on company programs as being all that is required. In a later chapter we discuss other roads to self-improvement.

Each institution which has been around for a while has a normal or typical progression path for advancement, a path that usually varies depending on specialty, i.e. the route in a brokerage house or bank or a museum will be different from that in a manufacturing company. Find out what the accepted path is and set some goals for yourself. In the small organization there may be no "typical path", but the question is the same," What do you have to know or to have demonstrated in order to be ready for the next couple of steps?" Then establish the program required *with dates* when you will have met the requirements. This doesn't mean you will get the promotion or transfer at that time, but it does mean that you can be ready when the chance comes. It also means that when your boss has a "How'm I Doing" talk with you (see Chapter 8), you will be ready to discuss your ambitions and to get his or her suggestions about how to accomplish your aims. One of the steps will be to have a qualified replacement in place and ready to take your position.

Choosing a "hero" whom you wish to emulate, someone whose career has elements that appeal to you, may be a real help. Try to analyze why your hero has been successful and what qualities and experience you need to emphasize or develop in order to follow the same path. Try especially to find out what this person was doing at the same career point and age that you are.

If the opportunity presents itself, it is often wise to move back and forth between line and staff jobs. Taking a staff job where you can be working with an executive you particularly admire may give you an intimate view as to how that person functions. In addition staff assignments often result in working at a higher level in the organization than would be possible in a line position. The opportunity to see and understand what goes on at the higher level may tell you what weak points in your own experience need to be bolstered. In any case the balance of seeing the operations from both points of view gives valuable insights.

In the chapter on Getting The Most Out of Your Own Talent (Chapter 19) we are reminded that the successful athlete or star musician keeps practicing and you must keep polishing your skills as well. Don't be satisfied with just doing your job in the 8 or 10 hours a day it takes, but consider the "extra" that will prepare you for the "varsity" when the chance comes. This is particularly important in the small organization where each job may have several facets.

It sometimes happens that a particular company situation is such that it just isn't possible to work your career plan. I'm not talking about having chosen the wrong corporate culture, but rather the situation where your path is blocked indefinitely. If there is no way to solve the problem inside the institution by, for instance, moving to another division or transferring to another location, then you must decide to leave and go to a new job. This obviously is not a step to be taken lightly and always involves the risk that the situation you don't know is worse than the one you know, but there are times when it is the only solution. When you do decide to look outside, you must tell your immediate superior and where appropriate, you must also tell that executive in the institution who is recognized as being in charge of organization and development. (This person is not always in the Personnel Department!) You may learn that your perceptions were wrong and that your career path is in fact working out. You may also learn something about yourself that will be very valuable even though you must look for a new position if that continues to be necessary. You may also learn that you have failed to communicate your desires for a job change and simply getting the idea out in the open is all that is required. For example, the problem may be your own failure to develop a satisfactory replacement. Of course the better the people you have working for you and the more trained they are in their jobs, the easier it is to bring in a replacement and thus the more likely it is you will be able to follow your chosen path. This is why you must always get the best possible people working for you.

Your career is *your* responsibility. Others may have a stake in it and others certainly influence the precise details of how that career unfolds, but no one has the same interest that you do and no one can do more than make opportunities available. It is up to you to be ready when the chances come, and it is up to you to make your own success.

CHAPTER 18

LET'S GET ORGANIZED

Getting organized is really not so difficult. Let me list the elements and then discuss each one of them.

> A good Secretary
> A "To-Do" list
> A Calendar
> A Wastebasket
> "Discuss With" Folders
> A "Chron" File
> Project Files
> A "Black Book"
> Check Lists
> A Telephone
> A Computer
> Some Good Habits

We'll be talking about these elements one by one and how they work together.

First on the list is "A Good Secretary". If you rate a secretary, having the best one you can get is an important step in getting organized, however, in this day and age many managers don't have a secretary or at best must share one with others. In Chapter 10 we talked about how to work with a secretary if you rate one. Until that happy day comes, you will just have to do the job yourself!

Next to having the best possible secretary the most important aid in getting organized is the routine use of a "To Do" list. The form which the list takes is not particularly important. If your job requires that you be on the move, an ordinary 3x5 or 5x7 index card or equivalent is a handy way to keep the list. It can then fit into a pocket. At your desk just a pad of paper in the top drawer will do the trick. The method is simplicity itself. Just write down those things that have to be done as they come up and cross them out when you have taken care of them. Some people feel it is wise to "prioritize" the list a couple of times a day, but that really isn't necessary. You *know* the relative importance in any case. What *is* necessary is to keep adding new items as they come up. This is one of the "Good Habits" you must establish. The very act of writing down what has to be done speeds up your getting work taken care of. Later in this chapter I shall be discussing the use of the sub-conscious mind. Listing what has to be done starts the subconscious even as you go about other tasks.

But you say, "I can remember the things I have to do and I don't need to bother with any list." In practice that statement just doesn't hold up, or you will find you are spending too much nervous energy trying to remember what a piece of paper will never forget. If you want to be really fancy, all this listing can be done through a program on a computer terminal or on one of the electronic notepads. I'll have more to say below about using the computer in getting organized, but as far as keeping a "To-Do" list, electronic gadgets are no more effective and far less portable than a piece of paper! And a piece of paper never goes "dead" at the wrong moment!

After the "To-Do" list, a calendar may be the most useful tool. You should maintain one large enough so a month at a time can be seen and with sufficient space for each day so the daily schedule can be written in. These are readily available at any office supply store. A calendar should not only show appointments with associated blocks of time, but you should be able to see at a glance when reports are due or other deadlines which must be met. This latter includes your travel schedule with times of departure. Your appointment calendar should run out a year in advance and be of good enough quality to become part of your permanent files. It is very useful to be able to go back three or four years and pin-point a particular meeting or trip.

You must also have a pocket calendar to carry. There are plenty of different types available and you should choose one you are comfortable using. Again, get one of good quality so it doesn't fall apart half way through the year and so it can become part of your permanent files. It should be obvious that having your own pocket calendar means you can confirm future appointments right on the spot rather than having to call your secretary or wait until you get back to the office. Depending on the nature of your job and how much time you spend at the desk, you may be able to get by with just the pocket calendar.

The WASTEBASKET is put in caps because it plays a greater role in getting organized than you might think. Use it! Not only is it important as a way of getting rid of junk mail, but it is the first line of defense as far as your desk and your files are concerned. As Edwin Bliss points out in his book *Getting Things Done*, "If your office is typical, roughly three quarters of the items found in your files should have been placed in your wastebasket". Don't keep anything around your desk that you are not going to use or, after reading it, you can get from some other source when you do need it. If it is something you just want to read, put it in your briefcase to read at home or on the plane then put it in the trash can. Don't load up your files with material you don't intend to refer to. The wastebasket isn't known as the "round file" for nothing!

One of the most useful techniques is the use of the "Discuss With" folder. You should maintain such a file for each person whom you actively supervise or with whom you regularly work including your own boss. It's probably most effective to keep these folders within easy reach in your own office. That way as thoughts occur to you, you can drop a note in the appropriate folder. Each file should have a "To Discuss" list very similar to the "To Do" list and the file should also contain memos, notes or other items you want to talk over with the person. Such a file coupled with a regular schedule for meetings is not only organized and efficient, but it makes for more productive exchanges. The very decision to put an item away for future discussion clears the deck for more urgent things and once again, starts the sub-conscious working.

Let's stop for a moment and talk about the **sub-conscious**. Don't underestimate the power of the sub-conscious mind. It is a powerful tool for solving problems and for coming up with the "bright idea". It works while you sleep or while you are doing something else thus adding to your effectiveness. When there are too many problems to be resolved or when no satisfactory solution to some particular problem seems to be at hand, just putting the problem in the back of your head and going about your business will start the sub-conscious working. Surprisingly one is often aware that the sub-conscious *is* at work because possible answers or solutions will pop into one's head at odd times until a satisfactory one appears and is *consciously* accepted. Sometimes jotting down the thoughts as they appear will clear the way for more.

Closely related to the "Discuss With" folder is the "Follow Up" file. (This file has different names in different organizations: Suspense File, Tickle File, Date File, Reminder File, but they all have the same function.) If you have a secretary, he or she should have physical custody of the file. It's purpose is to have brought to your attention on dates which you specify, items on which you wish to check progress or other wise take action. Your secretary (or you!) may wish to run 31 folders, one for each day of the month. At the daily meeting he or she should bring to your attention the appropriate items for the day. For weekend or other holiday, all the dates between the work days should be checked and the items either brought up on the day before or the day after as appropriate. All one needs do for the system to function is indicate on a memo or other item, "Follow Up 2/1/95" or "Follow Up Third of Each Month" or something similar. Not only does this technique free you from having to remember to check on something at a future date, it works like a deferred "To Do" list by calling your attention at appropriate times to a task that needs to be done as for example writing the monthly report. It is particularly useful when you want to check up on some item in six months or a year or even longer. There are computer-based follow up programs that will remind you by subject or by file of what must be done on a specific date, but they really aren't as satisfactory as the old-fashioned file where almost anything can be given a date and put in the file for follow up without scanning or special preparation.

Ordinary files are usually organized by subject. If you have a secretary, let that person do the organizing and hold him or her responsible for knowing in which file documents are stored. You should be able to ask for the "Perkins Report" and even though that report concerns computer installations and is filed under "Computers", your secretary should know where it is. Many secretaries maintain a log in which all incoming and outgoing documents are registered and disposition recorded. This is an excellent practice if used with some judgement to weed out materials of no significance. When you particularly want to keep certain correspondence in a particular file, just indicate by some agreed sign like "F-Labor Problems" what you want done. If you are doing the job yourself, you will be more likely to make good use of the "round file" and keep the filing to a minimum. Again with e-mail and computer memory, much of what you want to file will be on your hard disk or on tape, and you will want to make sure that back-up copies have been made.

Everyone should keep a "Chronological File". This file is in addition to the subject files and should contain copies in date order of every formal document which you generate: letters, reports, memos, minutes of meetings, whatever. This file will be part of *your* permanent record and acts as the ultimate index to your work product. No matter what happens to any of the subject files, your "Chron File" will have the record of your work so it can be found. If your files are computerized, be sure that one master back-up file exists as a Chron File.

A variation of the subject file is a "project file". When a specific project involves several categories each of which would ordinarily be in a subject file of its own, it may be better to keep the specific papers needed for the project in a project file. In fact you may wish temporarily to keep that project file in your own desk so you don't have to keep asking for it. Once the project has been finished or becomes inactive, you can turn the whole thing back to your secretary if you have one to be re-filed in the usual fashion.

For facts, figures and information to which you refer frequently, nothing beats the little "Black Book". A useful type is the kind that takes the many forms published by Lefax. These are punched for a six-ring binder and measure 3 3/4 x 6 1/2 inches, a convenient size to carry in a pocket. All sorts of pre-printed forms are available ranging from "Month by Month Daily" reports which are convenient for recording production or shipping figures to "Log-log" graph paper for plotting trends. Having such a Black Book enables one to record information instantly without having to wait for a clerk or a secretary to do it. It also is a convenient place for facts or figures one wants instantly available as when your boss asks you what yesterday's sales were! This is a particularly useful tool if you don't have a secretary or clerk because you can enter the information wherever and whenever it becomes available. As an additional advantage, developing the habit of jotting down useful information where it is easy to retrieve increases your own awareness.

A variation on the Black Book, or part of it, are Check Lists. Where routine or repetition are involved, rather than re-inventing the wheel each time, get organized with a check list. For example if you must be in charge of the Christmas Party each year, develop a list that shows step by step with dates what must be done for the party to take place. The first time you take on the job keep a record of all that had to be done with comment about how each step might be done better or with less fuss. Immediately after the function and while it is still fresh in your mind, dictate or write out a check list for next year. I don't want to belabor the point, but much in the life of any institution repeats whether it's the church supper or closing up the house for vacation. Anything that essentially gets done the same way time after time is a candidate for a check list. If the list is done well enough, the next time you may be able to just turn it over to someone else to do! In any case after an event which is likely to be repeated (such as the Annual Sales Meeting or the Trustees Dinner or Negotiations with the Union) sit down and write a summary of what went right and what went wrong. Put the summary in your Follow-up File for the next time.

There are many computer programs available which are really no more than sophisticated check lists. These cover everything from scheduling labor to business planning to doing your own income taxes. They are designed to take you step by step through some task. They can be useful mostly because someone else has done the work! Your own check list is easy to revise if you keep the original as a document in your computer's memory.

While we have been talking about very basic techniques of getting organized, the methods seem to be very "horse and buggy" in this day of multi-media communication highways! The electronic devices may be elegant, but they may not be the best use of your time. The chapter on "Where The Computer Fits In" discusses the limitations of computer programs and using computers, but in your own attempt to get the most out of the hours in the day, the computer certainly has a place. The important thing is to use judgement about what can and what cannot be done efficiently. If you find yourself spending hours interfacing with your computer for whatever reason, it is likely that you are not being the manager you should be. It may be better to stick to the Rolodex and the Black Book.

Handling daily correspondence is part of getting organized so let's take a look at that activity. To begin with your secretary should sort the in-coming material the way you want it before bringing it to you. He or she should also have removed from the Follow up File those items requiring attention. If you have to do the sorting job yourself, keep a wastebasket handy! Handle immediately anything that can be taken care of by just writing a note on the original document. Be certain to *sign* (or initial) and *date* the note. Next anything your secretary can take care of should just be handed back with whatever comment is needed: "Tell him, yes." "I'll see her next Tuesday at 10 A.M." "Please write for this catalog". You get the idea. Very often your secretary will write a more polished letter than you do. Some material should just be consigned to the Follow up File. If the exact wording of a memo or letter is critical or if the subject is so technical your secretary can't handle it, you will want to dictate. In many cases you can actually make better use of the time by writing the first draft in long hand or on your word processor and thus avoid several revisions. Using some kind of a recording machine or computer notebook can also be very effective particularly if you have to handle correspondence or write reports while traveling. Limit copies of letters, memos, and e-mails to those few persons who really need to know. Other people's time is important, too. Finally, when a matter is to be handled by telephone, jot down on the correspondence those points you want to cover then set the piece aside until you make the call. After the call, note the day and time on the correspondence and dictate or write whatever notes are necessary.

The end result of a session to handle correspondence should be your secretary if you have one taking back to his or her workplace for further action everything except those items on which you will be working or to which you wish to give further consideration. The more your secretary takes away, the better organized you are! Those things that you keep should go into an "Action" folder. One good way of handling this is to make the top drawer in your desk the "Action File". This keeps the work immediately available and acts as a constant reminder while keeping your desktop clear.

How you use a telephone contributes to being organized. Unless you have someone with you or are "concentrating" to meet a deadline, it is usually better to answer the phone yourself. Your telephone manner is important. Answering by name is a good technique. "This is Jones." tells the caller exactly with whom he is dealing. The tone of voice may set the tone for the communication which follows, "What can I do for you, Charlie?" while being friendly also gets to the point. Don't spend a lot of time talking about the weather or last night's game. That is also friendly, but it signals that you don't have much on your mind or much to do and the conversation is likely to be end-less especially if the other person doesn't have much to do either! The telephone is no way to discipline or to carry on an angry exchange. Those conversations must be held face to face. If such a sit-uation develops when on the phone, just terminate the conversation by saying something like, "We don't seem to be agreeing on this one, Susan, can we get together this afternoon at 2:00 to talk about it?".

If you are not answering the phone yourself because someone is with you, your secretary or whoever answers the phone for you should say, "He has Miss X with him, do you wish to interrupt them?" This allows the caller to get through with some vital mes-sage when appropriate. If you are concentrating and do not wish to be disturbed, make it a habit to tell your secretary from whom you *will* take calls. All others should be told, "He is not available just now. I'll have him get back to you as soon as he can." *Not* "He's busy." Everyone is supposed to be "busy"! If you have to answer the phone yourself and don't want to interrupt what you are doing, a quick, "Mary, may I call you back at 10:30?" or equivalent will mini-mize interruption. If Mary's message is really urgent, she will not be put off, but has the clue to be brief.

When you are not in the office, it is often effective for your secretary to say something on the order of, "I know she would want to talk with you, but she is not in the office at the moment. May I give her some message or tell her what you wished to talk with her about?" It may well be that your secretary can take care of whatever the caller has in mind. At the very least you will know what the call was about and can decide how urgent it was. The message given to you should always include the date, time and the phone number at which the caller may be reached.

Outgoing calls should be organized as well. Your secretary can have the usual message forms for calls to be returned spread out on your desk or on one of those desk needles. He or she can have typed out a list or entered the calls on a log sheet of some kind. Anything so long as the calls don't get lost. With "Voice Mail" the record will be available on the monitor. Jot down any points you want to cover and then make the calls. Calling back when people are less inclined to chat such as just before lunch or just before quitting time may well keep the conversation to the point! The same rules apply to calls which you originate as the result of your" To Do" list.

Now it's time to lay out some habits you want to develop. These are behavior traits which adopted by you will make all the other techniques discussed above that much more effective.

Date everything that leaves your desk.

Don't sign anything you haven't read.

Never send anything to your boss you haven't re-checked for accuracy and content.

Make every assignment carry a due date even if given orally, "May I have that by 3:00 this afternoon?" "Would you please do that first thing tomorrow?"

Routinely evaluate tasks in terms of pay-off. How many dollars are involved?

Avoid adjectives and adverbs. Use numbers.

Develop the practice of doing necessary background reading at odd moments when commuting, traveling or between meetings.

Make a habit of deciding not procrastinating.

Be frank and make clear statements.

Force decisions which they are capable of making back to your subordinates.

Get tasks or messages off your mind by sending handwritten notes to the appropriate persons. Winston Churchill was a master of this technique.

One last word—There is no substitute for clear thinking when it comes to being organized. Let me quote as an example a note written by Winston Churchill on July 17,1945 to certain members of his cabinet:

"In May I gave directions that 1600 doctors should be returned to civilian life forthwith from the Services. I presume these are already out, and I should like a report confirming this. The time has now come to make a further cut of doctors in the Services in order to ensure adequate medical attention for civilians in the coming winter. A further 1600 doctors should therefore be returned to civilian life by October 1. The proportion in which the three Services release these doctors should be the same as applied to the first 1600."

There you have it! This is the work of an organized person thinking clearly! Not a wasted word. A follow-up on a previous assignment, the background on the assignment about to be given to put the order in context, a specific order with *numbers* not adjectives, a date by which the assignment should be accomplished and a condition, but no detailed instructions to destroy initiative, under which the assignment is to be carried out. All done in less than 100 words. As the Biblical exhortation reads, "Go and do thou likewise!"

CHAPTER 19

GETTING THE MOST OUT OF YOUR OWN TALENT

Being a champion at anything requires continual work and practice. No one is surprised when the concert musician practices 5 or 6 hours a day, *every day!* We take it for granted when the athletes of a professional basketball team are out on the court shooting baskets every day or when the figure skater skates three hours in the morning and three in the afternoon. The champion golfer will make 500 chip shots just to get that extra edge of knowing the feel of the course. You should adopt this same attitude in your "profession" of being a manager/supervisor. If one wants to excel, it takes continual practice, "chipping away".

One excellent way to keep chipping away is to keep reading. As managers, executives or professionals we are fortunate today in having a vast resource of writings on the subject of management and on the specific technical aspects of almost any job. The very fact that you are reading this book is proof enough. When one thinks about it, there are at least four different kinds of material available.

Daily newspapers and the weekly or monthly general business magazines.

Technical, trade and professional journals.

Books

Videos and TV

DAILY NEWSPAPERS AND GENERAL BUSINESS PUBLICATIONS

It should be no surprise that as this is written, *The Wall Street Journal* has the largest daily circulation of any newspaper in the United States. The fact that so many find it wise to read the *WSJ* means that you should, too, if business is your field and you want to know what the others know! Of course the Journal is only one example and there are plenty of others. Every field has its widely read publication. For example *Restaurant News* or *Ladies Garment Worker* has all the latest news and gossip in their respective areas!

Let me digress for a moment to suggest how current publications should be read. Both newspapers and business magazines mix hard reporting with staff "human interest" articles. How much of the latter one reads depends on the subject and the time available. It may be entertaining to read Ann Landers, but it certainly isn't adding to your professional standing. The reporting of hard facts and current events are required reading, but even there one must always read with the shadow of doubt about how good the reporting is. The more one knows about a subject being reported, the more it is apparent that the reporter really missed the vital element or mixed up the facts which shouldn't be so surprising considering where in the scheme of things a reporter's job and pay falls. One should be especially careful about taking at face value what is reported on TV. Not only is having a report read aloud to you with commercials a particularly inefficient way to get facts, but TV is show business and even the best anchorman will shape the story to be sensational rather than just factual. In addition it certainly doesn't help your understanding of events to listen to what some "man on the street" thinks about what the Secretary of State is doing or what some child thinks about a major strike just because daddy is out of work! It may be useful for politicians, but it is of little real value.

In spite of the trash that is mixed in with the reporting, current publications and the TV or radio news do reflect current opinion and events on which one must keep informed if only to know why people are saying what they say. In general in reading daily newspapers one must allow for the biases of the staff and of the owners. On the other hand, the quality of good periodicals is reasonably high. There are many to choose from: *Fortune, Harvard Business Review, Business Week, The Economist, Dun's, Forbes Magazine*, etc. etc. What you do read is your choice of course, but by all means *read selectively*. Read with the aim of knowing what is going on that could be important to you. Look for the insight to judge opinions expressed by others. Skip all the rest of it! One good trick is to make a habit of cutting out items you believe are important and sending them to some of your co-workers. There are special little pocket knives just made for cutting out clippings. Don't hesitate to put something away in your follow-up file in order to check your judgement about what you thought was going to happen. The point is: one must read with the *intellect* engaged in order to profit from the effort.

JOURNALS

The second category of "Technical, Trade and Professional Journals" has a pretty obvious role. Not so obvious is what these publications can do for you when you take on a new job. Every time you get into a new job or a new field, find out what publications exist that specialize in the area. You will find the entire range from *The Seafood Leader* to *Factory Management and Maintenance* to *The Banker* to *PC World* to *Chemical Week*. Reading the appropriate publication not only teaches you the language of the trade, but also puts you at the edge of development in the field. You will get to know who the "movers and shakers" are in the specialty, what subjects people are concerned about, who the suppliers are, who the competitors are, and how to tackle specific problems. Again, as with the daily papers, read with discretion. You don't have to read every word of every issue, but begin to "absorb" the mystique as each issue comes in. Think about what could be applied in your circumstances. Perhaps there is an idea which you are not quite ready for, but which may work later. Cut out the article and put it in your follow-up file. Very often you will get a whole new concept or approach stimulated by an article you have read. As you get familiar with the sector, you will find repetition showing up since all business or non-profit activity is essentially repetitive. Don't be dismayed; just be more selective in what you read. You may even want to let your subscription lapse for a year and then pick it up again. The one thing you don't want to do is just let the publications pile up on your desk!

BOOKS

Most of all we are fortunate today in having a vast resource in the books on the subject of management which have been published since WWII. It is also fortunate that the basic nature of management practice, while greatly influenced by developments in communications, travel and data processing, really hasn't changed that much. The pace has changed, but the fundamentals have not. There is no need for today's manager to re-invent the wheel. There are plenty of books to tell him how to make one! Again, you don't have to, and you don't have time to, read everything, but there are a few classics which I commend to you. Read them aggressively looking for the nuggets that apply to your supervisory life. Incidentally, they make great companions for that long airplane ride.

> *My Years With General Motors*—Alfred P. Sloan Jr.
> Macfadden-Bartell 1965

> *The Folklore of Management*—Clarence B. Randall
> Little Brown & Company 1959

Parkinson's Law—C. Northcote Parkinson
John Murray, London, 1957

The Prince—Macchiavelli
Various editions are available

The Practice of Management—Peter Drucker
Harper & Brothers, New York, 1968

The Age of Discontinuity—Peter Drucker
Harper & Row, New York, 1968

Management—Tasks, Resposibilities, Practices—Peter Drucker
Harper & Row, New York, 1973

Innovation in Big Business—Lowell W. Steele
American Elsivier Publishing, New York, 1975

Managing Geographically Decentralized Companies—Geo. Albert Smith, Jr.
Riverside Press, Cambridge, MA, 1958

Don't be a passive reader whatever you do. Reading can be as much a waste of time as shuffling papers or watching television unless you force yourself to be aggressive about it. Challenge what the writer is saying! Compare with what you already know about the subject! Look for something you can use right away in your job! Underline the good stuff! Make marginal comments! Put that note away in your follow-up file! Pick up the combination which gives you a new approach to some problem that is haunting you. BUT KEEP READING! KEEP PRACTICING!

VIDEOS

There are a number of videos available for specific skills. Except for language training, I am not a great fan of videos because they take too much time. As contrasted to reading material, it is difficult with a video to change the pace of what is being offered or to skip to what one is interested in.

THE BLACK BOOK

I am a great believer in the "little black book", some way of writing down where you can use them, ideas and concepts which you pick up from whatever source. As you sit in a meeting, someone will make a statement that strikes you as full of insight. Write it down! As you read, extract ideas that may apply to what you are doing. When you come upon a schedule or a table of information which could be useful, cut it out and put it in your book. If the book can fit into your pocket, you can keep lists of equipment capacity, production records, specifications, authorities—anything to which you may want to refer. Not only does the book become a useful reference, but the habit makes you more observant than you might otherwise be.

EXERCISING THE INTELLECT

Another way to keep current in your field is to join one of the professional societies. Not only is this a good way to keep up with what is new, but it is a good way to get to know people in other institutions who share your interests. It isn't necessary to be a "practicing" whatever so long as the field interests you and you are willing to spend the time required to attend meetings. Just joining for the sake of adding an organization to your resume isn't worth it. Being active on the other hand is a good way to keep that intellect working. The contacts made in this way begin to form the network of friends who can be a resource of great value over the years.

Attending a night school or taking extension courses can be reward-ing. Most metropolitan centers offer excellent opportunities and many institutions will subsidize the tuition for courses that relate to your job. But don't let the subsidy be the only criterion. Take the courses you find stimulating which may be as much a question of who is teaching the course as it is the subject matter. It goes without saying that to be of any value you must be willing to dedicate the time required and that may mean a trade-off with an equal amount of time spent on the job. You have to make the decision, but the discipline of having regu-lar classes may mean that you will keep at it. If you study the careers of most successful executives, you will find they have at some point early in their career taken extra courses in order to fill in some specif-ic gap in their education. Think about it. Don't forget home study through correspondence or video courses. It takes more determina-tion, but the schedule is more flexible and you can go at any speed that suits you.

Finally there is the whole gamut of professional training offered by companies themselves or by such organizations as the American Management Association. When you get the chance, take advantage of it. The chance usually involves some sacrifice. You may have to con-tinue to do your regular job and get the work out even while attend-ing the session or it may mean coming in on Saturday morning. It may interfere with some extra outside activity like going skiing or attend-ing a family party. Whatever the trade-off, it is usually best to opt for the training. It is all part of being ready when the chance to move up comes along. The person with whom you are competing will probably be in the class! If it is an outside training session like those offered by AMA, in addition to the subject matter you have the opportunity to get to know people in other companies who are serious about their careers and who can be added to the network. These are people you want to know and the contacts are likely to be valuable in the future.

Self improvement is mostly a matter of attitude. If you go at each day and each task with the thought that there may be something to be learned, if you do your reading with your mind in gear looking for ideas or concepts which may be useful, if you are willing to make the sacrifice required to get that little extra in education or professional training, then the process need never stop and you *will* be ready when the chance to move up comes along.

CHAPTER 20

HOW TO GET PEOPLE TO UNDER-STAND WHAT YOU SAY

Managers spend a good deal of their time either telling people what to do, reporting to someone or addressing groups of people. No manager who is a poor communicator can expect to be very successful. Although we talk from early childhood until the day we die, practically everyone has trouble getting others to understand what has been said. It is a more difficult task than getting others to understand the written word or getting them to understand "pictures" because not only is the spoken word fleeting, but it often is heard as the listener wants to hear it which may be very different from what the speaker intended.

The spoken word is different in another way. As ordinarily used in person-to-person conversation, only enough is said for the other person to grasp the idea before he or she responds. Depending on the degree of familiarity with the subject, ideas can flow back and forth with only fragmentary sentences. Try reading a literal transcription of a conversation and you will see what I mean. On the other hand addressing a large group where there is no give and take means that complete thoughts have to be spelled out. Sentences must be long and complex in order to give the audience time to absorb what is being said and to give some body to the presentation. In "public speaking" as contrasted to person-to-person conversation the literal transcription when read seems ponderous. To prove the point try reading the speech of a great orator; it is hard to visualize that the speech could have stirred a large audience. Such speeches have to be read aloud, actually orated, to be appreciated.

All this preamble is to emphasize that oral communication, talking to others, is not simple and doing a good job at it requires thought and effort. The art varies with the circumstances and that is what we want to explore in this chapter. There are really three general situations under which one works when trying to *tell* somebody something rather than getting the message across by some other method. The three are:

> Addressing a large group in a hall or a room where you are the "speaker" and they are the "audience".

> Addressing a group around a table or some such situation where one is close enough to sense whether one has been understood. Business presentations are typically done in this manner. So are council meetings or committee meetings of non-profit organizations.

> Talking directly to one, two or say up to half a dozen persons in what is a conversational mode including a conversation by telephone.

THE LARGE GROUP

Let's take the first case first, addressing a large group.

Rule number one: **Spontaneity is out!** To get good results in putting across a clear message one has to prepare. The first step in the preparation is to ask the question, "Just what do I want people to remember of what I am about to communicate? What *is* the message?" Try to write it down in as few words as possible and in a simple statement. The next question is, "How much do they already know about the subject? Do they know enough to put it in context or do I have to provide the background?" Then comes the question, "What are the logical steps required to get complete understanding?" And finally, "What words must I use to be understood?" All this requires discipline on your part and requires some degree of written preparation depending on the circumstances.

The steps are largely self-explanatory, but a few words about a couple of them may be in order. In oral communication one dare not assume that the listener can jump from background to message without help. Even with a small group the logical steps to understanding must be supplied by you in sufficient detail and in language that every person you are addressing comprehends so that *all* will get the message. "Baby-talk" the reasoning! Where the audience is diverse and with different experience bases, it is obviously even more important. The old axiom with the large group is, "Tell them what you are going to say. Say it. Then tell them what you have said."

Let me repeat, the larger the group and the more diverse its composition, the more important it is to keep the message simple. Although sentences have to be complex in order to sound smooth and to allow the audience to keep up with your line of thought, words should be as simple as possible. The good, old, Anglo-Saxon ones are the best when it comes to carrying your audience with you. Large groups require uncomplicated ideas and simple aids: pictures, bar-graphs, pie charts and the like. Don't present acres of figures that no one can read and probably couldn't comprehend if he could. If you must use technical terms or "words of art", be sure to define them in simple terms for the listener who may have a different idea of what they mean. This is especially important when using letter abbreviations so commonly used in government lingo. For example, the first time you use "IRS" say, "I mean the Internal Revenue Service". The same practice should be followed for any other shorthand references that are not strict uses of the English language. It's a good idea to repeat the connection from time to time. Good TV talk show hosts are always careful to see that their guests define terms and so should you!

Most institutions have a language of their own for elements peculiar to their activities which is in such everyday use that all employees understand it. The problem comes when that language is used with an outsider! You may know that "RCA" means Request for Capital Appropriation, but your audience will think it is Radio Corporation of America! If you must use institutional terms, define them for your audience completely enough so they really understand.

If you plan to present material to be taken away by the participants, it usually is better to do so *after* your presentation otherwise a large proportion of your audience will be reading the material rather than listening to what you have to say, and they may be reading it with *their* vocabulary and definitions rather than yours. Speak slowly. There is excitement in addressing a large audience and a great tendency to speak too fast when the adrenalin gets going. (As I write this, President Clinton has this problem especially when reading from prepared text.) The modern sound system (when it's working, which must be checked in advance!) will correct for volume, but it only magnifies problems for the rapid speaker. Just because you are the world's greatest expert and familiar with what you want to say is no reason to rattle off your message at great speed. It may impress a few in the audience, but mostly it will turn the majority off and ensure that they will not be able to follow what you are saying. One way to pace oneself is to change pitch or volume and to repeat important thoughts.

> Let me repeat that. One way to pace oneself is to repeat important thoughts."

It doesn't hurt to stop talking, leave some space and look around at the audience (to see if anyone is paying attention!). Addressing a large group is rather like being an actor in a stage play. The "lines" have to be delivered so they are heard by all and understood even by the fellow in the second balcony. Since you can't see that person and judge how well you are reaching him, you must be especially careful. Since this *is* like being on a stage, another important principle is: take the time to check out the stage effects, the physical details, before the performance goes on.

> Does the light on the podium give enough illumination for your purposes?
>
> Is the sound system working properly? How is it turned on and off? Can the microphone be removed from its holder so you can walk around with it?
>
> Does the projector work? Who will operate it and does he understand the order of your material? If you control it with a hand control, try it out a few times so you know exactly how it works.
>
> Is there an extra bulb for the projector?
>
> Can the audience see whatever props you are using? Go to the farthest corner where there will be someone sitting and judge for yourself. Walk around to see if glare makes certain seats unusable. If using a screen, is it up high enough and big enough to be seen by everyone?
>
> Etc. Etc.

More presentations have been ruined by failure to check these little details than by failure of the speaker to perform! At least when your knees begin to knock as you are introduced, you will have the comfort of knowing the projector will operate and the microphone is on. By all means don't start off with something like, "I don't think most of you can see this chart—" Your audience will know you aren't prepared and stop listening. If something goes wrong, don't apologize profusely. Just take it in stride and do the best you can.

When addressing a group, there is no substitute for the "dry run". Go through the entire presentation, out loud, using all the props and preferably in the very hall which will be used. Have someone who will tell you "like it is" listen and criticize. Do your thing without interruptions at least once as a final test. One final word, NEVER READ a speech to a large group. It is perfectly permissible to read a single sentence or a paragraph where it is important to have the wording exact, but it is never permissible to read an entire speech even though you may have written it out in detail. We have all had the experience of a brilliant man hunched over a podium reading from sheets he is having difficulty seeing. It is a disaster! You should be so familiar with the content of what you want to say that even though the speech is there and you use it as a guide, it can be "talked" not read. To make it easier, just remember that it is *your* speech and no one else knows it the way you do! If it comes out different from the way you wrote it, only you will know.

THE SMALL GROUP

The second situation of the small group gathered around the conference table is one with which most people deal often. Not only does one have the advantage of a more homogeneous audience made up perhaps of familiar individuals, but certainly one can tell almost immediately whether the message is getting across. However, just because there *is* the possibility of individual interaction, one must be sensitive to the mood of the group and tailor the presentation to suit. If you know of individual prejudices, address them or cater to them. If the boss doesn't like graphs, don't build your case on graphs even though it may show what you want to convey more clearly. Give the figures first and *then* show the graph. If the boss likes pie charts, use them. Don't bore your audience with things they already know, but do "baby-talk" the steps in your reasoning so no one jumps to the wrong conclusion. In this case it is permissible to use the "institutional language" without definition if all the members of the group are regular employees. When you sense that some idea isn't going across, stop and either ask a question which might clarify the point or repeat the reasoning in different words. On the other hand if the point has been made or the concept grasped by the group, move along swiftly. We have all had the feeling which comes when there is work to do and some member of the group just keeps talking!

Take the time to "test the water" if you come into a group that is already in session and has been working on some other subject. They may have been dealing with a disaster or a project which is far more important than yours and might have little patience for your proposition. If what you have to convey is good news, then there is not the same need for caution, but if the message is bad news or criticism, test before diving in! Maybe you would do better to come back at some other time if your project can wait.

Even with the small group, all of the rules discussed above apply. Know beforehand that the physical surroundings are correct and that all the equipment works as it should. Work from a properly prepared document or outline which has been "dry run" so you are comfortable with it. Anticipate the questions and be ready with the necessary documentation, but don't arrive with a mound of paper which you have to shuffle through to find anything. If needed, have it sorted and labeled so it is easy to handle. Have your calculator and any other displays or samples which may be needed. Hand-outs can be used with a small group, because you can control when to use them and when not to. In fact if the subject is complex and decision is expected from the group, it is best to distribute the necessary material well in advance of the meeting so that the participants have time to study it. If you plan to use lots of figures, always use a hand-out structured so it is easy to explain. Rather than have everything on one page that is solid with figures, it is better when possible to divide the figures into several logical segments presented a page at a time. Computers and

spreadsheets being what they are, it is easy to overwhelm the participants with figures.

Position yourself so you can see and address the maximum number
of people. If that isn't possible, be sure that you can speak directly to
the boss or senior member. The great advantage in dealing with the
small group is one can be sure the message has been understood.
Depending on the circumstances, it may be possible to direct questions
to the participants to be sure of the extent of understanding. Certainly
one can summarize in a way that invites comment and thus reveals
whether the message has gotten across. Whatever the technique, it is
your responsibility not that of your listeners to make sure everyone
has understood. Just think of each meeting as a little exam to be passed
with flying colors which you earn when everyone gets the message or
when you get the decision you wanted!

ONE ON ONE

In the more intimate situations of one on one or perhaps two or
three, interpersonal factors are more important than with larger
groups and there is more opportunity to "set the stage". Before delivering your message, think about the effect on the other person. Is this
conversation to be carried on across the desktop in order to add a little formality, or should you get out from behind the desk and sit down
together? Is the subject one that should be discussed over lunch? (I do
not favor taking a person to lunch to tell him or her they have been
fired or demoted! On the other hand lunch is a good place to work out
personal misunderstandings between equals or to decide on some
joint course of action.) Certainly a casual meeting in the hallway is no
place for serious discussion. Consider the chance of being overheard
and whether that is important before delivering your message in a
public place such as stopping by someone's desk.

Next think about timing. In most organizational situations timing is
determined by when a job has to be done, but quite obviously if the
message will come as a surprise, or if it is harsh or critical, timing can

be important. Friday night at quitting time is not a good time to deliver a message which will upset the recipient. Likewise if a serious negotiation is involved, it should be scheduled when there is plenty of time and little chance of interruption; not for instance when you have to leave for the airport in twenty minutes.

In most cases dealing with two or three individuals means there is far less chance of misunderstanding. However, misunderstandings do occur and often precisely because one doesn't expect they will and has been sloppy about preparation or because one assumes the message has been understood just because it has been delivered. Misunderstandings occur most often because the person being addressed doesn't *want* to hear what was said. Or it may be that he or she was too busy thinking about what to say next and just wasn't listening. One good way to be certain the message has gotten across is either to dictate a confirming memo once the conversation is over in the presence of the participants or to write up together a summary of the key items discussed. This has to be done while everyone is still in the room so that misunderstandings can be resolved on the spot. If you have prepared notes as a basis for the conversation, it is much easier to prepare the confirming memo. The memo doesn't have to be a literary masterpiece, but should contain date, place, participants and conclusions.

"At a meeting held in JWB's office on March 3, 1996 with JWB, GAB and RMC present it was decided:

1. To order the R7 copier

2. To install it in room 5

3. To pay for the copier and installation from funds left in the Office Supplies account."

Telephone conversations are a special case of inter-personal communication. The mistake made most commonly in getting thoughts across by phone is the speaker tries to be too clever! He or she believes that by circling around the subject and generating a nice warm feeling, the message, whatever it is, will be better received. What is more likely is that the message is *never heard.* Try this as an example. "How's it going, Bill? How was the golf game on Saturday. I understand you were driving them wild with your putts. Things are pretty busy down here today but you know how it is after the first of the month. What do you hear from the children...Is that so? I'm Just calling to say we expect to see you at 9 tomorrow morning. See you then." That's a friendly call, but how much better to get the message in the second sentence and to devote some time to the purpose of the meeting, where it will be held and who is likely to attend. After a clear understanding on the real reason for the call, if there is time, the conversation can go to the golf game. Again, if the message is complicated or important, it is well to confirm with a written note.

NET NET

Of all the modes of communication the spoken word is taken most for granted, but as any politician can tell you, when properly used, it is the most powerful of all. Proper use means most of all *proper preparation.* It means thinking through not only what is to be said, but how, when, and under what circumstances it is to be said. It may appear that many successful people do not pay much attention to the fundamentals set out here, but on closer look one will find that over the years they have established with great care patterns which have proven to work for them. You should do the same thing. The art of talking to people is basic to every job indeed it is basic to all our relationships with others. For the manager it may be his or her most important tool. Just one more word. If your job requires a good deal of speaking to relatively large groups, you may be well advised to take a course in public speaking. There are plenty of techniques proven over the years which any good instructor will teach you to use. Like any other skill, the experts have much to offer.

CHAPTER 21

WHAT TO DO WHEN YOU ARE MOVING TO ANOTHER JOB

This chapter is about a *voluntary* change of job. It is not about being fired or otherwise having to leave a position for reasons out of your control although some of the elements may have application in both cases.

When you leave the old job behind either to move elsewhere in the same company or to go off to a new employer, you can either let your successor worry about coping with what you leave behind or you can prepare the way. The latter option may gain you a life-long friend! In either case there are some things that have to be done for your own peace of mind. As soon as you know you're moving on, planning for the move can get under way. There are two distinct areas where action is required, those things you do for yourself and those you do for the company. Let's start with the things you are going to do for yourself.

If the move is out of the company or institution, you have to tell your boss before you start anything else. For obvious reasons you don't want your boss to hear about the great event from anyone but yourself. I'm assuming that you haven't been talking to the boss about "considering a move" and your decision is going to be real news to him or her. This will be no casual conversation so get prepared! You must be perfectly sure that the new job is a done deal. If there are any loose ends that might mean there is no job after all, don't talk about it.

Talk only when there is no doubt that you have the job (which means *having it in writing* in most cases) and you are going to move. If you really wouldn't mind being talked out of leaving, don't accept the *new* position until you have talked with your boss. If there are good and sufficient reasons to leave, accept the new job and then go talk with the boss. In the latter case it is really bad form to let the boss convince you to stay so you have to break your word on the new job. People do it, but it isn't honorable and it comes back to haunt them as part of their record. When you are ready to talk, what you want to tell the boss is the fact you are leaving and when you have to be on the new job. What you don't want to do is have a big session in which you get all your frustrations off your mind including telling him just what you think of *his* performance. He may try to find that out, but don't tell him! Concentrate the discussion on what has to be done to make a smooth transition and have a list of things you have thought about in that regard. Your leaving may cause more problems than you think, so give your boss time to analyze his problems by suggesting that he may want to postpone discussing the details until another time. Again focus on the actions required and stay away from the personalities. (Personalities may be appropriate for the exit interview, but not now!)

When the boss has been informed, the next most important decision from a personal point of view has to do with your immediate staff. This may be as simple as deciding whether your personal secretary, if you have one, is to go with you or to stay, or it may involve an entire team of people depending on the circumstances. If you are leaving the company, it is possible that you may convince your secretary to leave, too, but it is *very* unlikely that you should even consider trying to take anyone else along. If the job doesn't work out for any reason, you would have a tremendous responsibility to those whom you convinced to move with you. For a move inside the organization it is a different story and keeping a team together may be just the thing to do.

If you want others including your secretary to move with you inside the organization, you must promptly sit down with that person or persons as early in the game as possible and talk out the whole matter. It is your responsibility to see that those who move with you get as good a deal as they can as part of the package you are arranging. On the other hand if your secretary is to stay with the old position, the responsibility passes to your successor, but you should be sure your secretary understands where he or she fits into the picture. With other members of your staff the situation may be more complicated. Some working relationships are so personal that the new person may not be able to take over your team and keep its members productive. Perhaps this is a situation where you will not be able to take members of your staff with you even though they might expect it. In any case it is up to you to analyze the situation and to be frank with those persons who are directly affected. There are circumstances where you may have to tell one of your people to look for another job. If so, you must tell them far enough in advance of your own departure so you can help. Be realistic about your people. It really isn't fair to abandon someone who has been valuable to you, but for whatever reason won't be utilized by the new incumbent. Where others are to move with you, be sure to get the entire proposition down in writing and approved by the person who has the necessary authority. It is too easy to have misunderstandings when the agreement is verbal.

Having taken care of your people, you can move on to some other necessary tasks. Have an early session with the personnel department to be sure you understand the "conditions" with regard to insurance, pensions, savings plans, etc. etc. so you don't find out too late that you have failed to meet some deadline for conversion or that you owe extra taxes that could have been avoided by some specific action. Do this far enough in advance so you can plan the necessary steps. It doesn't hurt to have one session and then to come back in a couple of weeks to be certain you understood what you were told and that what you are basing your plans on is actually the case. This can be a bureaucratic nightmare so let the experts advise you. It is best in these matters to maintain the maximum flexibility. For example, don't cash out your pension plan or your savings plan if you don't have to and can take action later without any penalty. You have a lot on your mind and there are advantages to delaying such decisions until you have plenty of time to think about them.

Next it is time to work on the files. If you have, as recommended, maintained both subject files and a chronological file, arrange to take your chron files and your personal (having to do with your own private affairs) files with you. If there are files on disk or on tape, decide what to do with these as well. You should go through the confidential files and the files that contain correspondence with your boss and decide what to leave and what to destroy. Remember that confidential files which are left behind may not stay confidential for long. This may be particularly true with files in computer memory. As you review files, you probably will find project files or files dealing with subjects that are no longer current. These should be destroyed or sent off to storage in accordance with company procedures on records retention. The idea is to get the deadwood out of the file and to leave your successor with just those records he or she needs.

This is a good place to talk about the "Notebook". Once you start the process of leaving your job, you should start jotting down those things you want to tell your successor. Do it in a way that you can leave the notes behind with the new person, e.g. a small bound record book which can be carried around in the pocket is ideal. While you are going through files or as you go about your daily routine, write down those things you should pass along. You should also go through your follow-up file and make a list of those items or events with which your successor must deal and another listing those items on which you must *personally* follow up. In the notebook you may wish to devote a special section to the calendar or schedule, taking month by month and outlining what has to be done. Most organizations follow a fairly set pattern of events and each job has its own special pattern of regular events. Your secretary if you have one can do a pretty good job of developing such a calendar by reviewing yours for the last couple of years, but you should also review it and add to the list as required.

You should decide which furnishings are to go with you and how they are to be moved. You may not be aware of them, but there probably are procedures that have to be followed on the asset register to account for furniture or equipment that is moved. The building superintendent or office manager should know about the necessary reports and forms and will be pleased that you asked! Just don't get in the position of being embarrassed by not following protocol and giving the gossips something to talk about. Think especially about your desk chair. If it is really comfortable and you think it may be tough to find another as good, arrange to take it along.

Just as you cleaned out the files, clean out your desk and your bookcases or cupboards Now is the time to get rid of all that stuff you thought might be useful some day, but which never gets used. Be ruthless! This is also a good time to return those borrowed books and anything else that falls in the same category.

Next there are some things to do for the organization. Depending on the circumstances, there may be a number of outsiders who should be notified of the impending change before it appears in the newspapers or before you just drop from sight. Make up a list from your address file and decide whether a simple note will do to notify them or whether you should arrange for a face-to-face meeting between them and your successor. Your secretary should be able to develop such a list or at least get most of it. You should also consider notifying professional societies, clubs, and the like especially if your address will change as a result of the move. While you are about it, be sure to change mailing addresses on periodicals, etc. which should follow you.

Get out the personnel files on people reporting to you and review actions which should be taken on raises or other matters. You may want to hold up some routine increases so your successor can get the credit for giving them out and you may want to speed up some especially if they involve a special case or where you have made a commitment. You also need the review so you will be ready to discuss the whole file with your successor.

Go over your work plan to see if there is something your boss is depending on that should be finished up before you go. At the very least consider making a brief wrap-up report on where you stand on the work plan items so he or she knows the current status. You are going to want to discuss the plan with your successor. There may be elements that person will be expected to pick up and carry along to completion so a good review is required.

Finally, as you get close to the departure date, get out your schedule and follow-up file again and finalize for your successor the calendar which was started in your notebook. It is very useful to make up a list of "Things we do well in this department" and "Things we do poorly in this department" as a basis for part of the briefing of the new person. When these items are done, you are ready to sit down with your successor and have a session which will prepare him to step in. Following this session (to make this meeting most effective he or she should have read the chapter in this book on "The New Position") arrange to sit down with your boss to bring him up-to-date on what you have done and where matters stand. It is probably best to have this meeting *without* your successor present so your boss can ask whatever embarrassing questions he or she wants. However, at the end there should be a kind of formal session with the boss and your successor at which the "watch" is turned over. Depending on the situation, this may be no more than a brief handshake and good-bye.

A word of caution, there is no point in "burning any bridges" as you leave. Even if you have been waiting for an opportunity to "tell someone off" or finally to let someone know how you *really* feel about them, skip it! You may be back tomorrow and will regret ever having said anything. It is, after all, a pretty small world.

One last note. As soon as it becomes known that you are moving on, you will be surprised to find a significant change in what you are doing compared to what you were doing before the news was out. To begin with the time horizon moves in and most of what you have been doing for the future: next quarter, next year, no longer seems important and what's more those people with whom you work will no longer include you in sessions having to do with future actions. You will also find that your immediate subordinates (except those you are taking with you) will treat you somewhat differently. They may not check matters with you the way they used to, or they may not keep you as well informed about what is going on. In other words you will gradually be moved out of the system whether you like it or not. All this is normal and shouldn't upset you. What it will do is give you extra time that you hadn't counted on. Just use the extra time to be sure the move is done properly.

On your last day in the office, museum or factory, take the time to go around and say good-bye to people—and I mean *all* the people from the janitor on up. Let them know that you appreciate what they have done for you and that you respect them as individuals. Most of those people will be in the same place doing the same thing when you come back for a visit in five years. The least you can do is give them a feeling of dignity by including them as you leave the scene. It will make a big difference to them and it may make a big difference to you!

Part IV

USEFUL TECHNIQUES

CHAPTER 22

HOW TO TRAVEL AND ENJOY IT

This chapter is put into a section by itself because you will be using the ability to travel sensibly as long as you are able to get out of the house. What follows applies to men and women alike although I shall have some special suggestions for women who travel. Traveling is a skill every individual should develop. Don't fight it. Travel, at least in big organizations, is an everyday part of today's scene. No big deal the way it used to be since there is no place in the world more than 24 hours away by jet. Travel can be frustrating at best, but it needn't take nervous energy that you need for the job. The seasoned traveler takes in his stride whatever comes. He expects that things are going to go wrong at the least convenient times and has developed the ability to "roll with the punch". Of all the advice which follows, the most important is to avoid using your nervous energy on trying to reform the world you meet as you travel. If you need to vent your feelings about something, whip off a letter to the president or marketing vice president of whatever institution is annoying you and then relax! Just remember while everyone else is hollering and shouting you at least can be getting some work done.

Traveling is a lot easier if you keep folders or dockets made up for each of your regular destinations. The folder should have local maps, names of hotel personnel in hotels you frequent, personal information about your hosts, appointments, documents special to the location, telephone numbers, etc. etc. When you plan to make a trip to the locale, you or your secretary if you have one can pull the docket for your review and then put it in your travel case. It's good to be sure you have what you need. Your travel case should always have your passport (up-to-date and valid at all times) so you can leave the country from wherever you happen to be if travel overseas is part of your job. Also have a folder with a few office essentials like letterheads, postage stamps, spare cartridges for your pen, whatever you need to feel comfortable on a sudden trip out of range of your office. Keep "frequent flier" stickers and similar materials in your case. Your secretary or your spouse should have a record of numbers of your credit cards, driver's license, air tickets and traveler's checks plus a photo copy of the first pages of your passport that show number, date and place of issue etc.

The cardinal rule of successful travel is: **Don't trust anyone!** to get it right; not your secretary, not the travel agent, not the ticket agent, *nobody.* They all try to do their job and this is not to say they didn't mean to do it right, but, after all the arrangements have been made, you **personally** must check all the specifics. Do the tickets have the proper destination? Are the hotel confirmations correct? Is the rental car reservation included? It only takes a minute, but it is essential before you leave the premises to start the trip. If anything goes wrong, you are the one who is *really* inconvenienced! Have everything in one folder, your **Travel Docket**. It should contain details of your schedule hour by hour, confirmations of your hotel reservation, confirmation of rental cars, airline tickets, conference tickets. The whole trip in one place. Then "check it out yourself". Don't forget the expense account form! Keep it up-to-date as you go.

The second rule is: **Never get separated from your luggage.** With a little planning you can even travel around the world with only carry-on luggage. That may sound a little extreme, but the hours spent waiting for bags to be delivered are all wasted. Only *one* instance of losing one's bags for a couple of days will prove the principle. There is one exceptional case and that's when you are traveling with your spouse which means you will be responsible for two persons. In that case if you *are* able to limit to just two bags, pack part of the basic essentials in each bag so if something happens to one, you both can continue to function.

But it isn't only on airlines where the principle applies. When traveling in a caravan of autos, always see that your luggage is in the auto in which you are riding. I don't have to tell you which auto gets lost and doesn't make it back to the plane if *your* bags are in it and you aren't!

HOTELS

This is a subject well worked over by other authors. For the business traveler the main attribute of a hotel is to provide a good night's sleep. Mostly you don't care about much else except the ease of checking in and checking out. If you are in town only briefly, the airport hotels may be your best bet. Why waste two precious hours getting in and out of town when all you really want is a little sleep? The shuttle service provided by airport hotels is also a great convenience.

Rule number three—**Never trust a hotel wake-up call!** Always carry your own alarm and set it yourself. It's all right to use the hotel call as a back-up, but if you depend on the hotel operator, the best is that you wake up every couple of hours to see if the call should be coming in. The worst is that the call never comes after you've finally gone into a sound sleep and then you are wakened by a telephone call from your first appointment wondering where you are!

Rule number four—Be serious about checking out the fire escape routes particularly in overseas hotels where an emergency will bring excited people speaking a language you don't understand. The rest of what to do in case of fire has been published many times, but remember, *use the stairs and not the elevators.*

Here are a few more specifics:

Hotel reservations must be for guaranteed late arrival and with written confirmation. With that piece of paper in your hand, no hotel clerk can get by with saying there are no rooms left even if you have to sleep in the manager's office. Incidentally, never accept a room over the bar or the dance floor unless you don't want to sleep.

Don't spend any time arguing with a desk clerk in case of trouble. Get the manager right away even if it means a telephone call in the middle of the night. You don't have to be excited about it. Just say, "It's obvious that you aren't able to handle this problem so please just call the manager!" In many cases the clerk *will* be able to handle the problem rather than get the manager out of bed.

For national chains, if you have difficulties, don't hesitate to write headquarters with your problem. They are concerned not only about you, but about all the rest of your organization's employees. They don't want to risk being black-listed.

Use all the special privilege cards available to you. Again, chains are serious about trying to make customers out of the frequent traveler. You might as well get in on the goodies.

If you want food in a hurry, especially breakfast, it is often best to walk across the street to the local coffee shop. Most hotels believe you have unlimited time for meals especially breakfast!

AIRLINE TRAVEL

In this day and age there is very little difference between airlines although you may develop some individual preferences based on your own experiences. Usually the choice is made strictly on the convenience of the schedule. If one airline fails you or develops delays, go to the next and don't let loyalty mess up your schedule. You can be sure that very few people involved in your airline scheduling will have any imagination. You'll have to supply that ingredient yourself. Learn to use the Airline Guides. Don't hesitate to specify an unusual combination of flights if it will accomplish some purpose even when told by the counter assistant or the computer, "We never do it that way." An extra hour of flight time or a strange connection may save you a whole day for business.

Probably the most important thing in air travel is always to ticket ahead and, if possible, get a seat assignment as the reservation is made. Let your secretary or travel agent know which seats you like in the various types of aircraft. In any case get a boarding pass and a seat assignment as soon as you get to the airport if you don't already have them. Airlines have a habit of over-booking and the individuals with boarding passes and seat assignments are the ones that go on the flight for sure. Some airlines insist on your checking in at the gate and do not issue valid boarding passes except at the gate even when your travel agent has provided you with a boarding pass as part of the ticketing service. Just be sure that you understand the rules and check in as soon as you can wherever you have to, and then go about your business. Here is one place where being a frequent flyer can be of help. The computer at check-in will show your status. Frequent flyers get upgrade coupons, access to special lounges, early boarding and being put at the top of any waiting lists. I urge you to use the "perks" you can get. (If you purchase tickets online, most airlines give you extra mileage credit)

Here are a few other tips:

> On an over-booked flight, once on the plane with an assigned seat, stay there! It's their problem, not yours. Just don't get off the plane because the door may close behind you!

> If your flight is cancelled while you are at the gate, grab your airline guide and get on the telephone with the carrier to get a new reservation and thus beat the rush to the counter. There are usually more reservation clerks available by phone than at the counter.

Avoid seat assignments next to the galley or the toilets especially on long flights. The crew thinks the galley is a private club just for their amusement and the conversation and laughter never stop. If you have long legs, avoid seats next to the bulkhead. On some planes only midgets can be comfortable in a seat facing a bulkhead. In any case, airlines love to put mothers and children in those seats. The next seat will likely be occupied by a frantic mother and a tired baby. If you don't want to cope with children…!

On the plane be explicit in your instructions to the flight attendant about such things as whether you want to be disturbed for meals etc. etc. Especially on overnight, trans-oceanic flights, the crew likes to awaken the whole plane early so its job can be easily completed before landing. You don't have to eat breakfast if you don't want to! Telling the crew, "Wake me half an hour before arrival." may get you an extra hour's sleep in case of headwinds or other delay.

In the off-season on long distance or trans-oceanic flights life in Tourist Class or in Business Class may be a whole lot more peaceful than in First Class even if you have the chance to fly First Class (very few experienced business or professional people travel first class any more. It is basically an accommodation for "personalities"). If what you want to do is work or sleep, the first class schedule of drinks, dinner, movies, snacks etc. etc. is not for you. Remember, the next day on arrival the crew quits working when you start! Three seats together in Tourist makes a better couch than anything you'll find in First unless you book a berth. Business class is a good compromise if your organization can afford it.

One last rule, when the airlines start serving free drinks, you know the delay is serious!

AUTO, TAXI AND LIMOUSINE

Travel by auto, taxi, limousine, or rental car has its own hazards. To begin with everyone agrees that the statistical chance of accident is much higher in the auto than in other methods of travel especially when one is tired or suffering from jet lag. So beware. Don't try to do too much if you are doing the driving after a long air trip especially if you are in unfamiliar territory.

The first rule about rental cars is: if you are traveling with someone, let them rent the car even if you intend to do the driving. Any subsequent problems of mechanical trouble, check-in, billing, etc. etc. will be his and not yours.

Again, take advantage of all the privileges which are offered to get your business: upgrading, pre-booking, special status etc. etc. If you don't, you will be last in line on arrival because you will have been identified as the occasional user.

The next rule has to do with the use of individual limousines. "All limousine drivers are a little stupid". Don't ever trust them even in their own territory to know the way to your destination. Don't hesitate to give the driver orders. He may look formidable in his uniform, but he's working for you. Go over the map with him *before* you start off. In many cases it is worth getting a map ahead of time from the person you're going to see; or get his secretary on the phone on arrival and have that person give the driver the necessary instructions. In very difficult situations, have a guide meet you on arrival at the airport to lead the driver. Limousine drivers have a great habit of going off for lunch or gasoline or whatever, just when you want them. Be specific. Tell your driver, "Don't leave, I may want to go on at any time." If there is mechanical trouble, don't hang around while the driver tries to fix it. Either the company promptly sends another limousine so you can continue, or just call a taxi and get on with the show. If the limousine company has not fulfilled its contract because a car broke down, don't pay!

Finally, limousine drivers tend to be great conversationalists. You don't have to listen to them. If you are alone, it is a good time to get some work done so long as you keep one eye out to be sure the driver hasn't taken a wrong turn and is on his way to getting lost. Just say, "I'm sorry driver, but I have some work to do to be ready for this next meeting."

The good driver expects and is worth a reasonable tip at the end of the day. This should not be routine, however. If your driver has done a poor job for any of the reasons suggested above, make your tip reflect it.

Taxi Drivers are in a class by themselves. In certain big cities they are famous for trying to take advantage of the traveler. Especially at airline terminals, stick to the regular cab companies and cab lines. If you are doubtful about your destination or about the charges, ask the starter. In many places there is a flat fee from terminal to town. In others the meter runs. If your destination is an out-of-the-way place, have a clear understanding with the driver *before* you start the trip. Again, the starter will help you if you are uneasy about what the driver is telling you. Where possible, using hotel shuttle services is a better bet than taxis. By and large the same thoughts which apply to limousines apply to cabs. Usually there is little problem. It is generally better to let the driver choose the route even when you are familiar with the territory. They know what the current traffic conditions are. If you know the difference between the "scenic" route and the regular route, you may want to tell the driver which you prefer. Just don't get taken for a "ride".

It should be apparent from the references to "getting on the phone" that having a cell-phone if you expect to do a great deal of travel is almost a necessity. Even in places where telephone service or pay phones are available, having your own phone saves you from having to stand in line or having to cope with the procedures of some phone company you have never heard of !

OVERSEAS TRAVEL

Most of the rules about traveling in the United States apply to overseas travel—only more so. For example, the rules about pre-planning and confirmed reservations are even more important. To the extent you can, always have reservations in writing so there is no doubt about accommodations. Most reputable hotels are now reachable on the internet and getting confirmations does not require any delay.

Essential to any travel, *but most important overseas,* is the availability of money. Fortunately, the more common credit cards work in every language. Be sure all yours including your telephone credit card are in good standing before you leave home. But credit cards will not pay for a taxi or a tip to the porter. In fact you can't do much outside the hotel in any country without local currency. Get some before you leave the airport. Usually the exchange rate is better there anyway. Even better, if you are a frequent traveler, is to carry enough for immediate needs as part of your regular travel kit. There are special wallets available with pockets for several different currencies. (Can you imagine trying to get on a bus in New York City without U.S. money—or trying to pay a New York cab driver with Italian lire?).

In spite of all the ads to the contrary, carrying a certain amount of cash is a good idea. Cashing travelers' checks or using credit cards may have red tape connected with the transaction with which you don't want to cope. But the ads are right about the security of travelers' checks so for modest amounts of money, say up to a couple thousand dollars, use travelers' checks. If you are going to need substantial sums for any reason, a letter of credit is the answer. Your bank can arrange it for you. (If they say they can't, get another bank!) Letters of credit are commonly used in Europe and South America and all good banks are accustomed to them. With a letter of credit there is a small initial fee, but you get charged for the money you use only as it is drawn down. Really large amounts of money are best handled by wire transfer.

There are plenty of good books about overseas travel and what to expect. They are well worth reading if you are a novice. One of the ones I like is *The Tropical Traveler* by John Hatt published in paperback by the Hippocrene Press in 1984. One piece of advice: do allow a little time in your schedule to see some of the high spots wherever you are. All work and no play, just isn't the way to go. There is a lot of stress connected with overseas travel and you will be more effective if you don't try to work seven days a week. You don't schedule Sunday work when you have visitors from overseas, and you shouldn't try to do it when you are the visitor!

Here are a few ideas you won't find in most books.

> Never eat raw shellfish! Anywhere! It just isn't worth it. There is no illness quite so acute or quite so violent as that caused by a tainted mussel or oyster!

> While most water in large cities is generally good, use water from the hot water faucet for brushing teeth or for drinking. Hot water has basically been pasteurized in the process of becoming "hot water" even though it may be cool out of the tap. Ice cubes on the other hand are very likely to be contaminated.

> By American standards, coffee in the rest of the world is strong. Ask for a pot of hot water to dilute it; drink cafe au lait; drink tea; or whatever—just don't underestimate how strong the local brew can be. Go a little slow on the social cup of coffee offered as you make your visits. After a half dozen cups, you will either be "flying" or at very least have spots before your eyes.

A good sweater is a most useful piece of clothing on an overseas trip. Not only is it very comfortable to wear in the plane, it may save your life during a cold snap or when worn to bed on a cold night. Heating is not too well done in much of the world.

Don't argue with officials, and don't volunteer information. Just answer any questions the best way you can. Even if you're competent in the language, stick to English and let them worry about the exact meaning. When you're excited, you may just use the wrong phrase in a language foreign to you.

You'll have to fill out lots of forms. This is no place for trying to be funny. Just answer the questions as simply and accurately as possible. Anything else is likely to result in a long interview with immigration or the security officials. They have *no* sense of humor!

Guard your passport with your life! You may have to give it up from time to time, but understand why it is necessary to turn it over and where the document will be in case you need it, as for instance if you have to change plans. Have all the details written down in your wallet or some safe place in case something happens to your passport i.e. Number, date and place of issue, etc. etc. Don't just leave your passport in your hotel room. The best thing is to keep it on your person or otherwise with you when you are out of the United States.

Get your sleep! Jet lag is tough to deal with and the best cure is to take a nap whenever you get a chance. Keep up the vitamin pills and the liquids. Plane travel is dehydrating. Alcoholic drinks just add to the problem since alcohol is a diuretic.

Unless there is no choice, don't go into a business meeting or any important event on arrival from an overseas flight. They will be ready, but you won't!

Watch out for the round of entertainment followed by negotiations. It's an old trick to have one team of people do the entertaining and another team do the negotiating while *you* burn the candle at both ends.

If you are able to do so, read the local newspapers and listen to local TV. There is much to be said for understanding what topics are of concern to the locals. It may save you from saying the wrong thing. In any case it helps get events in perspective and will act as a quick refresher course in the language.

Bedding may be strange in many parts of the world (Ever try to sleep balanced under a featherbed all night? It's a skill that takes years to learn.) Remember that a topcoat can be an extra blanket and can anchor other bedding in place. A coat with a zip-in, down-filled lining is particularly good. Wearing a sweater to bed is an old trick which has been proven by generations of travelers.

Always reconfirm airline and hotel reservations as you go. Just because you have a ticket for a flight doesn't mean that you are in the computer and that your flight is confirmed. In general national airlines are more likely to be on time from their home country than those passing through. In case of mechanical trouble, the national airline is more likely to have the needed spare parts on hand. e.g. Lufthansa in Germany, Air France in France, Quantas in Australia etc. etc. The point is, use the local airlines even for the next overseas leg if you are able to and have no prejudices.

Carry an ample supply of medicines and toilet articles. You can always get them in an emergency, but the procedure especially in the case of prescriptions is likely to be involved in spite of what American Express says in its ads. Be sure to have an anti-diarrhea medicine as part of the kit.

Getting a new prescription usually means finding a local physician who will write it for you. Going to the emergency room in a hospital is another good source. In most places there will be an English speaking doctor available in the emergency room. Good hotels are quick to help and have physicians on call.

As pointed out at the beginning of this chapter, certain basic office supplies are well worth carrying. Certainly you will want a refill for the pen or pencil which you customarily use, but a couple of letterheads, some scotch tape, a small stapler, a couple of sheets of carbon paper and some envelopes can also be very useful. A battery for your calculator or for your pocket organizer is a good idea. They are often difficult to match. If you need your laptop computer, be sure to have an extra power package!

Remember that the power supply outside the United States is likely to have different voltages and frequency. Carry a multi-purpose transformer if you will be using the local power supply.

I personally like a hard-sided suitcase of the Samsonite variety. They don't look like much, but they will take tremendous abuse. On the other hand, soft-sided, vinyl bags are easier to stow in overhead racks. Watch out for bags that depend on zippers to keep them closed.

Zippers have a way of giving out at the most awkward moments. Be certain that the handles are tough and comfortable. By the time you have hauled a heavy bag the whole length of Charles deGaulle airport you will be happy the handle holds!

Luggage should have locks!

TRAVEL IN THE TROPICS

Travel in very hot climates has its own set of hazards. Probably the first problem comes when you climb down out of an air-conditioned plane into the hot sun of your destination. Don't underestimate just how bad it can be. Stay out of the sun during the middle of the day until you are completely adjusted. As Noel Coward put it, "Only mad dogs and Englishmen go out in the mid-day sun."

Keep the liquids up! Iced tea in places where you can trust the water is excellent. Be careful about alcoholic drinks which can be deceptive in hot climates. Bottled waters or orange drinks are good so long as you can trust the source. International names like "Perrier" are sure to be good. It is most important not to become dehydrated. (Remember, Ice cubes can be made from contaminated water!) Again, keep taking vitamin pills. They help in the change of diet.

Clothing has to be loose-fitting and easy to wash. "Jockey" style underpants are likely to cause rash or infections. Change to one of the looser, boxer types. Stockings should be acrylic rather than nylon. Cotton is fine, but cotton stockings don't wear well and they take a long time to dry once wet. Nylon tends to be hot. Leather sandals are good for leisure, but be sure they are comfortable for walking (Your feet are likely to swell in the tropics.). Composition soles are better than leather which is prone to mildew.

Light colored garments are better than dark because they reflect the sun's rays.

Malaria is a real danger in many parts of the world. Ask the question! If you are going to a part of the world where malaria occurs get an anti-malarial drug and start taking the pills *before you go* and *keep taking them* for as long as your doctor recommends. Remember you can get malaria just by changing planes in an airport if it is in malaria territory. It takes just one bite from the mosquito carrying the disease to transfer it.

Check with your doctor about other possible shots to be taken like cholera or typhoid. The tetanus shot should be active. Just because these diseases have pretty much been eliminated in the U.S. doesn't mean you may not run into them particularly when traveling in the tropics.

Be very careful about eating. Since fruits are not washed, it is better to prepare your own, i.e. order the whole fruit and prepare it yourself. Avoid the obvious things like cold meat salads drenched in mayonnaise. The reason why foods in tropical countries are so often highly spiced is that the spice conceals the fact that the underlying meat is tainted. For some persons the spice alone can't be tolerated. Breads, pastas, any dish which has to be well-cooked in its preparation, are safe. Look with suspicion on salads, uncooked vegetables and especially shellfish.

This is not meant to be an extensive medical treatise, but one other warning about the tropics is in order. Even the slightest cut has a way of getting infected. Don't take any chances. Use an antiseptic and bandage if you get cut.

A SPECIAL WORD FOR WOMEN

Most women who travel have no more difficulty than men and everything which has already been written in this chapter applies. Nevertheless, women do have to take some common sense precautions mostly having to do with security. Here are a few tips:

> Dress modestly and in accord with the customs of the region where you are. Especially outside the United States dress should be very conservative.

Don't wear fancy jewelry. Keep a business-like appearance in all accessories.

Airport hotels are usually security conscious and make a good choice especially because they can be reached by shuttle buses or directly from the terminal. Otherwise, in metropolitan areas a small hotel known to a friend or to the travel agent may be a better choice than the very large, mid-town institution.

In the large hotel make sure the front desk clerk doesn't call out your room number when you check in. If it happens, tell them you don't like it and ask for another room. When going to your room for the first time, use a bell-hop.

Never leave the door of your room ajar. One is likely to do this if luggage must be sent up or if expecting room service. Don't!

Make sure the door closes and locks properly. Use the night safety. That's what it's for.

Verify by phone to the front desk any request by the staff or a repair person to come to the room. If you don't know who it is, don't let them in.

Before leaving the hotel, check with the concierge or the front desk to find out about the neighborhood and areas to avoid. Don't go out alone unless absolutely necessary and *DON'T WEAR A BADGE WITH THE MEETING OR ASSOCIATION NAME ON IT.* IT IS A SIGNAL TO EVERYONE THAT YOU ARE A VISITOR.

If you need to use a rental car, try to get one with no identification on it. Like a badge, it is a signal to everyone that you are a visitor. This is especially true with airport rentals.

If you have a rental car (or your own car for that matter) and require directions, either get them before you leave the rental desk or stop at recognized gasoline stations. Overseas it is best to stop at the police station or at a highway toll booth.

Traveling in the tropics is even more difficult for women than for men. In addition to the tips already outlined above, use your own common sense in choosing clothing and shoes that you know are comfortable in the hottest days of summer.

If taking a taxi, let the starter help you and have him give the driver instructions.

At the airport or in the train station stay with the crowd. Don't wander off into a dimly lighted arcade or shopping area.

In Italy and many Latin countries, beware of the police and the military. They like to harass women and consider it perfectly proper behavior.

If staying at a motel, ask for a room near the front office preferably in the same building block with the office and the other amenities.

If you want to have a drink, it is better to take it in the lobby area, patio, or restaurant rather than the sports bar or whatever passes for a bar in the hotel. Overseas, most good hotels have two bar areas, one of which is arranged as a sort of sitting room where women are expected to take their refreshment.

In elevators, it is best to be with a group of people or with someone you know. If you are late and really concerned about going to your room alone, don't hesitate to ask the bellman to accompany you.

NET-NET

In today's international environment everyone is likely to have to travel. With some attention to detail and a proper frame of mind, travel can be quite pleasant. The horror stories one hears usually are the result of carelessness on the part of the traveler or of the unwarranted expectation that all systems will work and all persons are responsible. There is not much point in using up energy by getting angry when things go wrong. Instead just focus on finding a solution to the problem. If you have done all you can and are just waiting for events, you might as well get some work done. On the other hand, when things are going right, take the opportunity to look around and to enjoy what the world has to offer wherever you may be.

CHAPTER 23

DOING BUSINESS OUTSIDE THE UNITED STATES

This chapter is written both for the person who may actually be involved in doing business outside the United States and for the person who may be involved in making decisions about such business or who just wants a better understanding about what is involved. The technical professional may find this description useful in dealing with foreign visitors or when making a foreign visit. Even more it is hoped the chapter will be valuable to the new manager who may be asked to take on an overseas assignment.

The business world really knows no boundaries although it must cope with the artificial barriers set up by politicians. What the commercial world *does* recognize are differences in needs and tastes of customers. To be sure, there will be many specific local differences in the way business is done, local accounting requirements, local regulations, etc. etc., but any business that is carried on in more than one location in the United States faces many of these same types of local differences. It is relatively easy to determine the factual things like rules and regulations that must be complied with. Where most enterprises go astray in trying to do business outside the United States is in meeting the requirements of unfamiliar customers.

With the above as a preamble, how does one go about getting into business outside of the United States? There are usually three phases in a successful effort:

Export from the United States

Joint venture for local manufacturing or sourcing of certain products, usually the less demanding ones.

Setting up a wholly owned venture.

The most important single element in making a success of an overseas effort is the naming of at least one competent individual who will have no other responsibility than seeing to the overseas thrust and who will have access to top management. It goes without saying that making an overseas effort must have real support from the top. There is always a great temptation to add the task on to someone who has expressed interest in expanding the market horizon, but who already has a demanding domestic job. As a result the overseas effort is made in a "stop and go" fashion: a flying trip to the country in question, a hurried conference at the end of the day, a telephone call from home at night or on the week-end...but always *after* the demands of the "regular" job have been met.

The person to spearhead the overseas effort need have no prior overseas experience, although such experience is obviously helpful. He or she needs know no foreign languages although again a working knowledge of one or more can be very useful if only in making the person more comfortable in a foreign situation and in helping establish personal relationships with foreign associates. The person must, however, have the confidence of his superiors when it comes to business judgment. They *have to trust his judgment* since second-guessing will abort the whole process. One cannot carry on business outside of the United States on the basis that everything has to be referred back to the home office for approval or on the basis that an agreement in principle will in effect be renegotiated by someone back in the States.

The second step is to choose the most favorable market for the original effort. Developing an overseas enterprise is going to go slower than expected in most cases, and there is always the voice at the home office who is not too enthusiastic about the idea in any case, so the market where some near-term potential exists is the one with which to start. As the effort continues, repeat sales of any magnitude can be a three or four year proposition. Don't be misled by macro-economic reports about where future opportunities lie or some newspaper article sparked by some political development. What you want is a market that exists right now. For example, as this is written, the papers and journals have been full of the trade potential in China with its huge population and awakening economy, yet China is probably the last place for an initial effort by someone interested in export markets. As a general rule, Canada or a European country is the best place to start. Canadian markets are quite similar to those in the United States and barriers to trade are few. Mexico is now favored with the advent of NAFTA although regional differences may be more pronounced, but there are still substantial difficulties except in the big cities since the economy is quite fragile. For Europe the access from the United States by jet is easy; English is widely used and understood; the commercial scene is settled and well-organized; currencies including the new "euro" are relatively stable in relation to the dollar and to each other; and trade channels are well-established. But don't make the mistake of trying to take on all Europe to start. You wouldn't go for national distribution in the United States for beginners. Don't do it in Europe either. Choose a well-defined area where your product has potential (this usually means limiting to one of the big four: France, Germany, Italy or the United Kingdom)and then choose the best market area within that country for the initial push.

Exporting requires *effort*. Your product may be a real winner in the United States, but if some version of it does not already exist in your target market, at least they have been able to get along without the product for all these years! This is going to take some hard selling on the merits. The first effort has to be identifying potential customers and understanding the competition. I don't want to insult your intelligence, but the job is done overseas the same way it is done here in the United States when you open a new territory. You *dig* for information. Let me point out that trade shows in Europe are a particularly good source of information both as to potential customers and as to competition. In some places the U.S. commercial attache can be useful, but frequently he knows less than you do. Let me also emphasize that you will not find out what you want to know sitting around the bar in the hotel talking to other business people from the United States! Local distributors who are already established are an easy way to start, but they may already carry competitive lines and in any case you must negotiate agreements which allow for future flexibility and change. When working with local distributors, don't go on the basis of an oral understanding. Rules about territories can be tricky and you are limited by the Commercial Code in many areas. Write down the understanding and get a local lawyer to look at it and tell you what limits there will be on future actions. Set an expiration date so there can be adjustments as required. What you don't want to find is that you must pay dearly to get back a territory from some distributor who is not performing.

Be prepared to modify your product or service to suit the local needs. One must be particularly sensitive to what must be done to satisfy the customer. There is a great tendency to believe that the market in the United States must be ahead of the market in other countries and, therefore, any request to change the U. S. product or its packaging has to be resisted; to say nothing of the fact that you will have to battle operating people to get changes made for an overseas customer. But this is exactly one of the reasons for starting into an overseas market through export. It gives one the opportunity to work out required changes and to determine the basic acceptance of a product before going ahead with local manufacture. Attention to detail and accommodation to local idiosyncracies is the difference between success and failure. You need the new customers worse than they need you. There will be many changes to be made. In Europe remember that metric system is used and your product should comply. Electric supply is 50 cycle and normal supply is 230 volts which means that motors and other components have to be changed from U. S. standards and so it goes. You really should translate your manuals and brochures into the local language. Don't try to get this done on an amateur basis by someone who has had a foreign language in school. Get a professional who knows the proper terms used in the trade and can make your manual sound like you know what you are doing. We have all had the experience of purchasing some item and trying to follow instructions written in pidgin English. It is pretty frustrating! While there is a growing similarity in taste between the U.S. and foreign markets, making the necessary adjustments is an important task.

The export phase can easily consume three or four years before one knows enough to take the next step. Usually it will be possible to do some local sourcing or joint venture activity during the export period, and if so, the additional effort may justify a local office which in turn will be the beginning of a local cadre of employees, etc. etc. In some cases due to the nature of the product or service, export is not possible and one must start with local sourcing. Care must be taken from the very beginning to keep the long run in mind in developing the relationship. If the long range objective is to have a wholly-owned foreign enterprise, local sourcing must be arranged with that end-goal in mind thus the source must not be a potential competitor. If the initial effort is to be a joint venture, there must be a buy-out formula as part of the deal. By and large, 50/50 joint ventures are not too satisfactory since in the long run the partners' interests tend not to be the same. There is always the temptation to show that one *really* trusts a new foreign partner by going for a 50/50 deal. Pure 50/50 ventures soon become headaches no matter how good they sound in the beginning. Certainly, one or the other of the partners should be in ultimate control. When a tough decision has to be made, especially when the partners don't agree, *one* partner must be able to say what the decision is going to be. If one must go the joint venture route for whatever reason, it is usually better to be dealing with a large company than a small one because the relationship is not quite so personal and emotions are less likely to enter into the business decisions. This is not to say that 50/50 ventures are not possible. Many successful ones have existed over the years, but they should be started cautiously and ordinarily should provide for a buy-out formula.

As pointed out in the chapter on "Working with a Lawyer", in the United States it is the practice to have long and detailed agreements full of "boiler plate". This is not the case in the rest of the world and agreements drafted in the United States are looked on with suspicion. Use a good, local lawyer who has the confidence of whoever handles your legal affairs in the United States and follow his or her advice. Often this will mean having a letter agreement signed by both parties rather than a complicated document. In many countries the Uniform Commercial Code supersedes agreements in any case, i.e. one cannot agree to something which is against the law!

I can't overemphasize the importance of taking a long view and being consistent in one's approach to the foreign market. An earlier article (1989) in *Business Week* describes the experiences of some companies who have been successful in tapping the overseas market and concludes that reaching a $10 million level of sales with a good product requires four to five years of sustained effort. They also point out that "Too many companies fold their tents and steal away when an initial sales blitz fizzles".

Now let's consider some of the situations one meets in actually transferring a business from the United States to an overseas location. In this case we are talking about an independent activity and not a joint venture with some established foreign entity. The following elements are essential:

> Personnel experienced in the mother-home knowhow must be made 100% available in the early stages so that transfer of detailed technology and operating procedures is properly made to the new operation.

Location of the new venture has to be determined with utmost care. In Europe this means taking into consideration the currencies and the workings of the European Community/Common Market as well as the physical location of major customers. There are real differences in labor costs and regulations in the different countries. As an example, with its strong currency, high cost of land, high cost of living, and advanced regulation, Switzerland is a tough place to locate a manufacturing facility, no matter how nice it is as a place to live! Don't be fooled by the euro currency and by the talk of a "United States of Europe". The real thing is not at all like the United States.

High-class, dedicated, local executives must be found, hired, brought to the United States and given training at the home location in order to form the cadre around whom the new overseas business can be developed. U.S. citizens can not be relied on to stay on foreign duty for any length of time. For that matter there are only a few nationals who seem to be content to live outside their native land. The Swiss, the Dutch and certain persons from the U.K. are notable exceptions.

Let's discuss these points. To begin with there is just no substitute for experienced people when it comes to transferring know-how. No manual, no detailed instruction, no amount of schooling replaces the in-depth skill of the experienced individual. This statement applies just as much to the successful salesman in a business where sales technique is important as it does to the technical engineer in a business which relies on a defined manufacturing process. There is a further advantage in using good U.S.-based people to transfer know-how. It creates in the mother company a nucleus of responsive, interested personnel whose reputation is somewhat dependent on the success of the foreign venture. The individual chosen for a temporary overseas assignment of this nature will always have empathy for the overseas problem and will constitute in the domestic company a focus of good-will for the overseas company. The overseas counterpart is much less reluctant to ask for help from a person whom he knows personally than to ask some mysterious "expert" whom he has never met. On the other side of the equation there is a certain unique quality in the experience of helping a foreign activity get started which gives the domestic employee a special kind of job satisfaction.

Secondly, the choice of physical location may have certain unusual elements involved. For some kinds of business there is not much choice. A chemical business that requires specific feed stocks may have very few choices as to location. For any business the location may be affected by the relationship of currencies and the importance of markets. One is often tempted to locate an operation in what would otherwise be an undesirable spot to take advantage of government programs involving tax abatements or outright subsidy. **Don't do it!** The reason why the inducements exist is that the knowledgeable, local people won't put businesses there without the special deal. If people who know the country need special conditions in order to locate in the area, it is no place for a beginner. I am talking here about the big programs sponsored by national governments, not the arrangements that can be made with a local city or county. Very often when the choice of location is down to three or four, the decision may well depend on what a community is willing to do in the way of roads, sewers, housing or local tax abatements. Housing can be particularly important in some parts of Europe or Asia since good people will not come if housing is of poor quality or non-existent.

Certainly before making any final decision as to location, one should talk with the local officials. They can either be extremely helpful or a great nuisance and it is well to know in advance! In spite of all you may have heard on the subject, don't pay any bribes to anyone to facilitate locating your business. It shows a certain contempt for the "natives" when you do so which they will not forget and it sets you up for future demands. (In any case, it is probably illegal both in the country and under the U.S. Foreign Corrupt Practices Act!) Your business should be able to stand on its own merits without any pay-offs.

Finally, choosing high-quality, local people to train in the United States gives an early sign that it is the intention to make a permanent success of the business. The quality of these people may give an "edge" in dealing with local officials from the very beginning. As pointed out above, sending U.S. citizens on permanent assignment overseas is rarely successful. Particularly where wives and children are concerned, it soon becomes apparent that the family does *not* want to stay overseas permanently and then the cry is to return "home" so that the children can be educated in the United States, get into proper social circles, etc. etc. As to the executive himself, he often thinks he has been forgotten by the home corporation as he sees his peers at home moving up in the organization and taking all the desirable jobs. Anyone good enough to spearhead an overseas operation will have both the talent and the ambition to be a top executive in the United States and thus will not long be happy in an overseas assignment. By choosing and training local residents good enough to build the business, one puts in place a permanent base for the enterprise.

In summary, success in doing business outside of the United States boils down to:

Selecting excellent people out of the domestic operations and seeing that they are 100% dedicated to the overseas effort. They should have no other job assignment while working on the overseas project.

Choosing a market for the initial thrust which is stable politically and economically.

Identifying customers and both establishing and measuring demand for products or services, preferably by export, until one is certain that the products or services have been adapted to the market.

When the business is sufficiently large and stable to justify a local venture, finding and hiring the best local personnel the company can afford and bringing them to the United States to be trained at the mother location. Nothing is more important to the eventual success of the enterprise.

Locating the physical plant with due regard to local practices and conditions. (Take the extra time to do this carefully since one is working in unfamiliar circumstances and a mistake can be very costly.)

Replicating the successful pattern in other markets once the first test has proven itself.

If the basic guidelines set out above have been followed, then all that is required is plenty of hard work and sufficient patience to make the work pay-off. As problems appear, one must be flexible enough to make the required adjustment. A manager doesn't expect circumstances in the U.S. to remain unchanged and there is no reason to expect they will in the overseas situation. The world is getting smaller and smaller as an economic entity. As economic union becomes the order of the day, no business should feel it has to be limited to the United States. The rewards are just too great when one learns how to reach out and to do business in the larger markets. Benefits flow along a two-way street with the feed-back from overseas often being of much value in the home market.

CHAPTER 24

HOW TO LOOK AT A FACTORY OR OTHER PHYSICAL FACILITY

This chapter is about a technique that not everyone will use, knowing what to look for and what to ask about in judging a manufacturing facility. The description is aimed specifically at a manufacturing plant, however, the thoughts outlined can also can be used as a sort of self-examination for the facility or department you are managing. Try it! For others who are not involved directly in plant management, the factors outlined in this chapter apply equally to a hospital or the physical plant of a school or any other institution which you may wish to evaluate. I will continue to refer to "factory", but you should think "any physical plant".

GETTING STARTED

Factories are the sum total of a myriad of details, little things, which tell the story about how well the place is managed. It all starts with the "signage" that tells one what the name of the company or institution is, where to enter the property, where to park the automobile and how to enter the premises. Are the signs legible, are they clean or properly painted and do they deliver the proper message to the stranger? It is surprising how often this first impression is a clear indicator of the condition of the entire enterprise! How about the parking lot? Are the visitors' spaces clearly marked? Does the lot reflect discipline and thought? Is it clean? If there is a lawn or shrubbery around the lot or the entrance, has it been properly cared for?

Once through the door is it clear to whom one should address inquiries and does that person understand that an important part of his or her job is to act as receptionist? (One of my pet peeves is the factory entrance into a small office with three or four people working at their desks who, until finally spoken to, *ignore* the visitor as though each were trying to avoid having to deal with the "intruder"). If an attempt has been made to have a reception room or area, is it clean? Is the furniture in good repair? If there is a display case or bulletin board, are the items on display current and can the visitor decide what they represent and why they are on display? Nothing is more damning than a bulletin board with product literature or other publications which are obsolete, dusty and faded.

TOURING THE FACILITY

Once the tour starts, your attention will be mainly focused on the purpose of your visit i.e. why did you want to make the visit in the first place, but you should look for some or all of the following indicators as part of your overall judgment:

> What is the "tone" of the place? Do people appear to be friendly and purposeful in what they are doing or is there something sullen about the mood?

> What is the pace of work? Do you get the feeling that the place is humming or is the impression too relaxed? Are some persons apparently doing nothing or do they only pretend to be active as you walk by?

Take a look at a factory bulletin board. Are the messages dated and are they up-to-date? Is the board neat or is it a mess? Are the messages legible?

What is your impression of the general lay-out? Does work appear to flow naturally or is there a lot of trucking back and forth? Is there a great deal of work-in-process inventory all around? Is material in process labeled or identified? It doesn't hurt to pick up a batch card and ask your guide how the system works.

Look up at the ceiling. Is insulation torn or missing from the piping? Are all electrical fittings closed and no hanging wires? Are pipes properly supported without wire pipe hangers? Is the area clean and properly painted? Are things orderly or is it a jungle up there? One can tell more about the level of maintenance in a building by looking *above* normal eye level than by almost any other device.

Look down at the floor. Is it clean and free from defects? Is the floor surface being torn up by wheels of hand trucks? Are aisles and storage areas marked off with proper lines?

This is a good time to ask your guide to explain how maintenance is done in the plant. Does each department have resident mechanics working for the department manager or is all work assigned out of a central pool? Who determines which jobs get done first? Is all work strictly craft work or can a mechanic use a pipe wrench? How do people feel about the quality of maintenance?

Make your own judgement about maintenance. How does the electrical work look? Is it clean cut, in straight lines and in conduits where appropriate—or is it all over the place? How does the pipe-fitting look? Are joints leaking? Do steam traps work? Any visible steam leaks? Is insulation in place and guarded where it should be? If there is carpentry, are the joints true and square and are structures tight? If machine adjusters or mechanics are at work, is the place a mess or does the work appear organized? Do machines have proper guards in place? Are repairs professional or is there evidence of "bailing-wire"? What do the tanks and pressure vessels look like? Any leaks? Is the paint in good shape? If there are measuring boards, are they firmly attached and legible? Is there an inspection record on the pressure vessels? How about the instrument panels or boards? Have all the charts been changed? Is the board well laid-out and labeled?

Where drums and boxes are stored, are they in straight lines looking as though they had been put there on purpose? Have the corners of stacks been protected against damage from forklifts? Does everything appear to be coded legibly?

Look at the work stations. Do they show evidence of industrial engineering in the lay-out? Are parts fed from proper bins? Does work flow to and from the position in a natural pattern? In a multi-story building does work flow from the top down?

Where computers or terminals are in use, is the area orderly and is the equipment properly protected?

In taking a tour through an entire factory, it is usually best to follow the process from beginning to end rather than taking it piecemeal as it comes. Ask your guide or host if it is possible to start with the receipt of raw materials and then follow through to the finished good storage. Ask questions about where the raw materials come from, who specifies them and who tests to see if they meet specification. Ask how sampling is done and what happens to rejected materials. (Are they marked and stored so they can't possibly be used in error?!). As you move through the process or operation, continue to ask about quality control and sampling procedures. This will often tell a great deal about where the trouble points are. If you want to get an idea about how reliable certain stages of the process may be, keep asking about rejection rate or spoilage at the various steps. Verify by looking for scrap or rework. Remember, yield is cumulative. A 90% yield at each of three stages in an operation is only 0.9 x 0.9 x 0.9 or 73% overall. Ask your guide to tell you what happens to scrap and other rejected material. Is it salvageable? It is often possible to verify what you are being told by speaking to an operator. Keep your question simple but leading, "Do you get much spoilage in this operation?" or "What's spoilage been running—around 10%?". Many times there will be figures posted on bulletin boards or on signs showing production or yields. Be aware! Signs may also tell you where the trouble spots are. In any institution the management is likely to put up signs for matters which are sources of concern.

Look under stairs and in corners to see the level of house-keeping. Check a fire extinguisher to see that it is properly tagged and inspected. What do the hydrants or hose connections look like? Are hoses available and are the outlets clear or are they blocked by stored materials?

Check the accuracy of scales by stepping on the platforms and weighing yourself. Is there a tag showing when the scale was last inspected? Ask your guide who checks the scales and how they do it.

Ask to have the hourly-rate incentive program explained. What kind of safety program do they have? Are safety posters used? What is the most common accident?

Think about the level of illumination and the type of lighting fixtures used. Good illumination is essential to hand work and inspection, but it also adds to the general tone of any operation and at very little cost.

If there is a chance to look over a roof area (especially flat roofs), see if the condition is uniformly good. Is there any puddling? Are the drains working properly? Any debris on the roof? Ask whether there are problems. (This is particularly important for museums or libraries where water damage to the collection can be disastrous.)

If outside, take a look at window frames especially steel sash. Are they warped? Are they free from corrosion? Any broken panes?

What is the condition of the exterior walls? Does the brick need pointing? Is drainage water led away from the foundations? Any evidence of corrosion of reinforcing steel or spalling of concrete? Any debris or clutter around the buildings?

Look over the factory or administrative offices. Are they neat and orderly or is everything a jumble with papers piled high on desks and filing cabinets over-run with records? A factory office should be immaculate!

A visit to a factory property should not only be a chance to evaluate, but also a chance to learn. Look for "good ideas" to take back to your own plant. Getting the most out of a factory visit requires real energy input. If you just put your mind in neutral and placidly listen to your guide, it may be more relaxing, but you won't get much out of the visit. Generally speaking people are proud of their knowledge. By making the effort to get actively involved and by asking lots of questions, your guide will respond, you will see much more and better understand what you have seen thus putting yourself in position to make some informed judgments.